Writing Works.

using a genre approach for teaching writing to adults and young people in ESOL and Basic Education classes

by Marina Spiegel and Helen Sunderland

Learning Unlimited
Institute of Education
20 Bedford Way
London WC1H 0AL
Tel: 020 7911 5561
Email: info@learningunlimited.co
Web: www.learningunlimited.co

Printed and bound by CPI Group (UK) Ltd, Croydon, CR0 4YY

Acknowledgements

The authors would like to thank the following:

Hazel Hirshorn, Maggie Roberts and Stuart Roberts for the picture stories and Sally Hancox for cartoons

Students whose work has been used and adapted for the writing extracts

Sarah Freeman and Sue Colquhoun for trialling the exercises and giving us valuable feedback

Foufou Savitzky for proof-reading and suggestions

Maria Morales and the ESOL team at New Vic for getting us started

David Wray and Maureen Lewis for the idea of writing frames

Our families for patience during our fruitful but lengthy collaboration (particularly on Sunday evenings)

Lesley Jacobs for her administrative support

Rachel Fletcher for the design

Colleagues at LLU+, Richmond Adult and Community College and Kingston Adult Education Service for their support and ideas

London South Bank University for making it possible

ISBN: 9781872972541

Shirani

Contents

Contents table

Contents table continued

Genre	Reading	Text Analysis	Language Features	Writing
3b Narratives (Intermediate)	• reading for overall meaning • reading for inference	• characters, events, setting, outcome • irony • 1st and 3rd person narratives • differences between spoken and written narratives	• adverbials of time • chronological markers • use of adjectives • pronoun referencing	as 1b
4a Folk Stories (Foundation)	• reading for specific information	• writer's purpose • introduction/middle/conclusion • who and where • traditional beginning and ending	• traditional phrases for beginning and ending folk tales • regular and irregular Simple Past • punctuation: direct speech & common verbs	as in 1a
4b Folk Stories (Intermediate)	• skimming • reading for inference	• introduction/middle/conclusion • traditional beginning & ending • use of tense	• punctuation: direct speech • relative pronouns	as in 1b
5a Formal Letters: Explaining (Foundation)	• skimming • reading for specific information	• formulaic opening & closing • first and last sentences • order of ideas • differences between spoken and written explanations	• giving reasons using because • use of can and could	as in 1a
5b Formal Letters: Complaining (Intermediate)	• scanning for key words • reading for specific information	• formulaic opening & closing • first and last sentences • order of ideas • differences between spoken and written complaints	• use of conjunctions: and, but, as, because • useful expressions • prepositions of place • use of Present Continuous + still	as in 1b
6a Applying for Work (Foundation)	as in 5b	• formulaic opening & closing • first and last sentences • order of ideas • differences between spoken and written applications	• vocabulary for job seeking • useful expressions • for/since with Present Perfect	as in 1a
6b Applying for a Course (Intermediate)	• predicting • reading for specific information	• purpose • beginning & ending • content & order of content • use of tenses • differences between spoken and written statements	• useful expressions • contrasting use of gerund and infinitive • use of Simple Present, Simple Past, & Present Perfect • spelling: advice/advise practice/practise	as in 1b

Contents table continued

Introduction

This book sets out to adapt and use some of the practical approaches of genre theory to the teaching of writing to ESOL and Basic Skills students in Britain today. The book has 9 units exploring different types of text or genres: descriptions of people, descriptions of places, personal narratives, folk stories, formal letters, applications for jobs and courses (personal statements), reports, discussion essays and comparative essays.

A brief account of genre theory and the debate and controversy which surrounds it is given in the Appendix at the end of the book.

Each unit follows a similar format: the units are divided into 2 parallel sections, one at foundation, the other at intermediate level with 2 'model' texts at each level. Each section then contains:

- a short set of reading exercises
- 1 page of text analysis
- 2 pages of language exercises
- 1 page of writing exercises
- 1 writing frame

Four sections also include mind-maps, and letter layout templates are given with the formal letters in Unit 5 on page 68 and 76.

Using the Book

The approach we advocate in using this book is based on the results of practice in the classroom by the 2 authors and colleagues who have helped to pilot the materials. It is a teacher's book and not intended for self-access by students. We do not believe it is appropriate for use with beginner level ESOL students, as the meta-language expected for the text analysis and the writing exercises is too demanding.

For each genre we recommend the following stages:

1 Oral Modelling/Presentation and Practice

Oral work linked to each genre should precede all literacy activities. That is to say that the presentation and practice of vocabulary, grammar, oral/aural and discourse skills need to be thoroughly explored prior to working on a given unit. Different presentation materials and approaches lend themselves to the different genres. For example: photo or pictures as stimuli for describing people and places, taped folk tales, a group discussion with 'for' and 'against' teams, role playing interviews for a course. Oral work not only introduces and practises vocabulary and language structures which are generic to a text but helps students focus on discourse features.

This is an important element in feedback following discussion or role play, even in foundation level ESOL classes, although here discussion is necessarily limited. At the intermediate level, oral work raises issues such as the structuring and ordering of information, cross-cultural conventions of presenting information, expectations of the participants and the importance of intonation, register etc. It is an opportunity to discuss differences between spoken and written usage. It is also a valuable time to explore differences between students' other languages and English.

2 Text

Following the oral work, students are given the texts to read. The short reading exercises focus on a range of micro-skills, for instance scanning or reading for inference. Teachers should ensure that any key vocabulary in the texts is pre-taught before reading them. The texts are offered as models for the particular genre, although they should not be presented as absolutes. We would strongly encourage teachers to bring in other examples of the genre

Introduction continued

to follow up the texts presented in the unit. It is also possible to extend the discussion by bringing in 'bad' or inappropriate examples for critical analysis.

3 Analysis of Text

A carefully structured section on text analysis then follows, with quite specific goals in mind. These include: the analysis of the writer's purpose and the function of the text, the organisation of the content, discourse devices that help achieve the purpose, conventions of written English compared to spoken English, comparison of cultural conventions between written English and the students' other written languages. At the foundation level, particularly with students who have a limited experience of education, it is important to teach the language of analysis quite explicitly and also to slow down or simplify the process. Experience has shown us that perseverance can lead to success. Mind-mapping, of which there are examples in the book in different sections, can be of particular help for foundation level students who are new to analysing text or to planning and ordering their ideas.

4 Language Exercises

For ESOL students, this section helps to focus and practice some of the key grammatical features for the particular genre. This section may need simplifying, extending or supplementing depending on the level of the students in the class. In some units both patterns and use are explicitly presented, but in others the language structure is less explicitly analysed. It is left up to individual teachers to decide what needs to be elaborated. It may also be that teachers identify other important linguistic features of the genre which they may want to focus on.

5 Collaborative Writing and Reconstruction of Text

This stage offers the students the opportunity to collaborate with both the teacher and their peers in the planning and drafting of their own writing. Students are often daunted by a blank page and need the support of a systematic structure. Teachers may wish to plan the first piece of writing as a whole group activity, alternatively students can work in small groups or in pairs to plan. The next part of the process offers a 'scaffold' in the shape of a writing frame to help students attempt their first draft. An important next element of this stage is the editing and peer discussion of the draft. At the intermediate level, students are asked to edit each others' work. This aspect of the process can be extremely valuable, though students need to discuss the fact that it is easier to be critical of the work of others than their own. In some of our classes, students have experimented with planning and discussing their drafts in their own language, writing their text first in this and then translating it. This has proved a very valuable activity for many of the students who have come to recognise the importance of authorship and the control of ideas through this experimentation.

6 Independent Writing

Students are encouraged to follow up their writing with an independent writing task in the same genre.

We hope you will enjoy using this book and that it encourages the development of writing skills among your students.

Marina Spiegel and Helen Sunderland

Describing Places

Text 1: Living in Brixton

1 I live in Brixton. Brixton is in South London and it is very lively and busy.

Brixton is a very multicultural area. My next door neighbours are from the Caribbean and upstairs there is a family from Chile.

I go shopping in Brixton Market. It has wonderful fruit and vegetables from all
5 over the world and is very cheap.

I like living in Brixton.

Text 2: Argentina

1 I was born in Argentina. It is a big country in South America, south of Brazil and next to Chile.

Buenos Aires is the capital. About 15 million people live there so you can imagine it is a very large city.

5 Argentina has many regions, with high mountains, rainforest and plains. In the south there are glaciers and it is very cold.

I hope to return soon because I miss my family and the sunshine.

Reading Exercises

1 Answer the questions

   1a Read the titles. What do you think the writing is about? What kind of things do you think the writer will describe?

   1b Now read both texts. Highlight words you do not know.

2 Do you agree?

	yes	no	don't know
2a The writer thinks that Brixton is a good place to live.			
2b She does not like the market.			
2c The writer thinks that Argentina is very beautiful.			
2d Buenos Aires is not very crowded.			

Text Analysis

1   Work with a partner

   1a   Look at texts 1 and 2 and find the introduction, the middle and the conclusion.

   1b   Answer these questions and discuss your answers.

Write the first sentence. Does it link to the title?
Text 1:
Text 2:
Look at the middle. Which paragraph is about: people, weather, geography, shopping?
Text 1:
Text 2:
Write the last sentence. Does it give new information about the place?
Text 1:
Text 2:

2   Think of other ways you could start and end Texts 1 and 2.

3   Describe a place you know well to your partner.

   Look at the difference between *telling* someone about a place and *writing* about it.

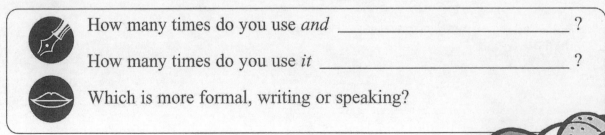

How many times do you use *and* _____ ?

How many times do you use *it* _____ ?

Which is more formal, writing or speaking?

Language Exercises

1   *in, from, next to, south of* are prepositions.
    Find examples of prepositions in the texts. Highlight them.

2   **Fill the gaps with a preposition.**

    2a Brixton is _____ south London.

    2b Wales is _____ England.

    2c England is _____ Scotland.

    2d Is Somalia _____ Europe?

    2e Where do you come _____ ?

3   *There is* and *There are* are very useful phrases in descriptions of places.
    Find them in the texts and highlight them.
    Complete these sentences using *there is* or *there are*.

    3a In my house _____

        _____

    3b In my street _____

        _____

    3c In Britain _____

        _____

    3d In the place where I was born _____

        _____

4   *It is* and *it has* are also useful in descriptions of places.
    Look at these sentences from the text. What does 'it' refer to?

    4a It has wonderful fruit and vegetables.

    4b It is a big country in South America.

    4c It is a very large city.

Language Exercises continued

5 Read Text 2 again. With a partner, discuss:

5a Where do you put a full stop in English? Is this the same as in your language(s)?

5b Where do you put capital letters in English? Is this the same as in your language(s)?

Put in the punctuation. Use a red pen.

> buenos aires is the capital of argentina about 15 million people live there
> so you can imagine it is a very large city argentina has many regions
> with high mountains rainforest and plains in the south there are glaciers
> and it is very cold

6 Put the words in the box under the right headings:

weather	history	geography	buildings
eg sunny			

cinema	mountains	old	hot	sunny	King	rivers	church
	capital city	shop	rain	battle			

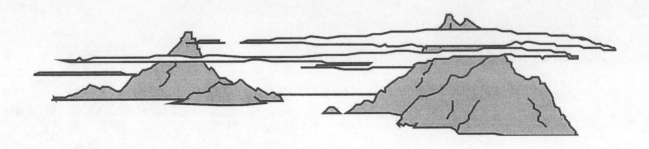

Writing Exercises

A good description of a place needs:
- to be written in paragraphs
- to have an introduction, a middle and a conclusion
- to have a good first sentence which introduces the place
- to give information about the place
- to show the writer's feelings about the place

① **Work with a partner or alone. Plan a description of the place where you live.**

1a First, decide what information you want to give:

name _____

where is it? _____

how big is it? _____

how many people live there? _____

what about the weather, history, buildings or any other things? _____

_____

what do you feel about this place? _____

1b Next, make a plan. Decide on the order for your ideas. Make notes:

title _____

introduction _____

facts about the place _____

_____

_____

conclusion _____

② **Write the description.**

2a Use the frame on the next page.

2b Now, read your description again. Are you happy with it?
Add or change anything that will improve it.
Check: spelling, prepositions, capital letters and full stops.

2c Lastly, write a final draft.

③ **Follow up**

Write about another place you know well.

Writing Frame

The place where I live

I live in _____

_____

_____

My neighbours _____

_____

In _____ there are _____

_____

and _____

It has _____

_____

I _____ living in _____

_____

_____

Describing Places

My Native Village

1 My native village is called Harangist and it is a small place in Somalia. It was built on the edge of a mountain facing the sea.

In my village there were about 600 people. We produced many crops like maize and tobacco and kept cattle. Many families lived by fishing. They fished all night in the Indian Ocean to
5 provide for their families.

People did not ask for much out of life and everybody helped each other. We had no electricity, no gas and no television – that is why we had large families. Water was taken from the village well. There was a school, a market and a mosque but no clinic. We had to travel to Kismayu to see a doctor.

10 We did not have many things in my village but we were happy.

My Country

1 I would like to tell you about my country, Cyprus. It is an island located in the Mediterranean Sea to the south of Turkey. According to mythology, Aphrodite, the goddess of beauty, was born on this island which is why its other name is the Island of Beauty.

Cyprus has a wonderful climate with four seasons. In summer the weather is very hot and dry
5 and in winter it is rainy and mild. For this reason the island is very green and covered in vegetation. There are two main plains on the island – Morphu Plain and Famagusta Plain. The first is suitable for growing rice. In Famagusta Plain one can see large orange and mandarin groves.

The island is divided between the Greek and Turkish communities. This happened because of
10 the civil war. I am Greek and I have never been to the Turkish side.

The first thing one notices on arrival is the many historical buildings, castles, churches, as well as theatres and cinemas. Visitors can also go to many beaches and enjoy the seaside. It is possible to fish and dive in the clear, clean waters which surround the island. There are many tourists who take advantage of its beauty and climate.

15 The tourists find that the people on the island are very friendly and hospitable and like to enjoy themselves, within reason. Cypriots love dancing and music. The thing I like best about Cyprus is the friendship and sense of community. I miss the laughter and sunshine and look forward to visiting my family and friends each year. In a word, my country is heaven on earth.

Reading Exercises

1   Read the titles of each text. What kind of things will the writers describe?

2   Read the texts. What is each text about? How do the writers feel about the places? Give reasons for your answers.

Text Analysis

Work with a partner.

1   **Find and mark the introduction, middle and conclusion in texts 1 and 2.**

2   **Discuss how the texts are the same or different.**

   2a   How does the first line in each text link to the title?

   2b   Read the introduction to each text. Is it a good introduction? Why?

   2c   Which text contains the following information: geography, farming, services, people, weather, history, tourism, culture?

   2d   How does each text finish? Is it a good conclusion? Why?

   2e   What are the main tenses used in each text? Why are descriptions of places sometimes written mainly in the past and sometimes mainly in the present?

3   **Look at paragraph two in Text 2.**

Look at the first line: It is a general statement about the weather.	*Cyprus has a wonderful climate with four seasons.*
Notice how the next sentence gives more information about the weather.	*In summer the weather is very hot and dry and in winter it is rainy and mild.*
Notice how the third sentence expands the subject further.	*For this reason the island is very green and covered in vegetation*

This is a common way to structure a paragraph:
1   general statement
2   specific information and examples
Find another paragraph in text 1 or 2 that follows this pattern.

4   **Describe a place you know well to your partner. Which is more formal, writing or speaking? Think about:**

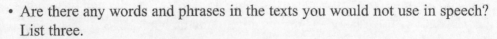

     • the use of *and*

     • the use of *it*

     • Are there any words and phrases in the texts you would not use in speech? List three.

     • How would you say these phrases?

     eg   People did not ask for much out of life. (written)
        We didn't expect a lot (spoken)

Language Exercises

1 **Read the expressions in the table and match with the description in the second column, saying how they are used:**

Expressions	How they are used in the text
My native village is called _____ *eg f* _____	a. to give further information
I would like to tell you about _____	b. to introduce the writer's opinion
The island is divided _____	c. to give information about the history
The first thing one notices is _____	d. to conclude
In a word _____	e. to introduce the subject
The thing I like best about _____ is _____	f. to introduce the place

2 **The above expressions are useful in describing a place. Find them in texts 1 and 2 and highlight them.**

3 **Work with a partner. Find the following structures in texts 1 and 2:**

there is	there was
there are	there were
one can see	
	we had
it is built on	it was built on

Highlight all the examples you can find.

4 **Fill in the gaps using some of these structures:**

eg *there* *are* two main plains on the island

4a _____ _____ _____ _____ the edge of a mountain, facing the sea.

4b _____ _____ a school, a market and a mosque.

4c _____ _____ no electricity.

4d _____ _____ about 600 people.

4e _____ _____ _____ large orange and mandarin groves.

5 **Find all the adjectives, eg *big*, in texts 1 and 2 and make a list.**

Do they make the texts more interesting? Can you think of others you could add to text 1?

Language Exercises continued

6   Give the opposite of these adjectives:

eg friendly *unfriendly*

wonderful	_____	new	_____
mild	_____	dry	_____
suitable	_____	clean	_____
hospitable	_____	happy	_____

7   7a Find the following words and phrases in texts 1 and 2:

and   but   for this reason   also

that is why   it is possible to   in a word

What do these words help the writer do?

7b Join up 2 halves to make a whole sentence:

eg   The weather was hot and dry   so they could provide enough food.

The town   for this reason I go as often as I can.

I love the cinema   *for this reason the island is very green.*

They fished all through the night   also has many restaurants and cafes.

It is possible to fish   but we were happy.

We did not have many things   and dive in the clear waters.

8   Answer true or false:

	true	false
eg to live is a regular verb, both in the Simple Present and the Simple Past	✔	
8a to have is an irregular verb, both in the Simple Present and the Simple Past		
8b to fish is an irregular verb, both in the Simple Present and the Simple Past		
8c to see is irregular in the Simple Past		
8d to be is a regular verb, both in the Simple Present and the Simple Past		

9   Using texts 1 and 2, find:

• 2 examples of regular verbs in the Simple Present

• 2 examples of regular verbs in the Simple Past

• 2 examples of irregular verbs in the Simple Present

• 2 examples of irregular verbs in the Simple Past

**10   Re-write text 1, using the Simple Present
      instead of the Simple Past as the main tense.**

Writing Exercises

A good description of a place needs:

- to be written in paragraphs
- to have an introduction, a middle and a conclusion
- to have a good first sentence which introduces the place
- to give information about the place in an interesting way
- to communicate the writer's feelings about the place
- to use the correct tenses, depending on whether the writer is talking about the place as it is or as it was

① **Work with a partner or alone. Plan a description of the place where you live. Use your own language to plan if you prefer.**

1a **First,** decide what information you want to give: name, location, size, population, weather, buildings, its history, special features, your feelings about this place

1b **Next,** decide on the order for your ideas. Make notes:

title _____

introduction _____

facts about the place _____

_____

_____

conclusion _____

② **Write the description.**

2a Use the frame on the next page to help you write the first draft, if you want.

2b Now, read your draft again. Are you happy with it? Add or change anything that will improve it. **Check:** spelling, verbs and tenses, prepositions and other grammar, capital letters, commas and full stops.

③ **Work with a partner and read each other's work.**

3a What do you think the writer feels about the place and why?

3b Is there anything that you do not understand?

3c Check it for the things in 2b. Remember it is always easier to find other people's mistakes than your own.

④ **Lastly write a final draft**

⑤ **Follow up**

Write about another place you know well.

Writing Frame

_____

I would like to tell you about _____

It is _____

_____

The first thing one notices is _____

_____

_____

_____

It is also possible to _____

_____

_____

_____

The thing I like best about _____ is _____

_____

_____

I hope _____

_____

Describing People

Text 1: My Daughter Emma

1 I would like to describe my daughter Emma. She is 10 years old and is my youngest child.

Emma is small and slim, with red hair and brown eyes. She has freckles and a cheeky smile.

5 She is very active and loves swimming and dancing. She is also bright and creative. She enjoys reading and painting. She has a strong personality. Emma is very stubborn and argues with me a lot. At school she is rather quiet. Her teacher says she behaves very well and is always helpful!

I am very proud of Emma and I hope that she will grow up happy.

Text 2: A Good Friend

Victor is one of my best friends. He lives just round the corner and our children go to the same school, that is how we met.

He is in his twenties and has got black curly hair and brown eyes. Victor has a dark complexion and wears an earring. He is from South London and likes to wear comfortable clothes, jeans and jumpers. He is of average height and of medium build. He is a driver and works in the evenings.

Victor likes to tell jokes and make people laugh. He is friendly but he can get angry when people are rude or cruel. We sometimes go to the pub together and I always enjoy his company.

We see each other a lot and I hope that we will be friends for many years.

Reading Exercises

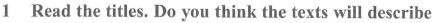

1 Read the titles. Do you think the texts will describe
   1a a place?
   1b a person the writer does not like?
   1c a person the writer likes?

2 Read the first sentence of each paragraph and see if you were right.

3 Read the texts carefully and highlight any words you do not know. Look them up in a dictionary or ask your teacher.

Text Analysis

Work with a partner.

1 Look at texts 1 and 2 and find the introduction, the middle and the conclusion

2 Discuss these words with your teacher or use a dictionary:
   age appearance behaviour interests occupation personality

3 Look at the table and discuss your answers.

Write the first sentence. Does it link to the title? Is this important in the introduction?
Text 1:
Text 2:
List the things the writer describes in the middle: Use the words from 2.
Text 1:
Text 2:
Write the last sentence. Does it give you new information about the person?
Text 1:
Text 2:

4 Think of other ways you could start and end Texts 1 and 2.

5 What tense do the writers use and why?

6 Describe a person you know well to your partner.

   Look at the difference between *telling* someone about a person and *writing* about him or her.

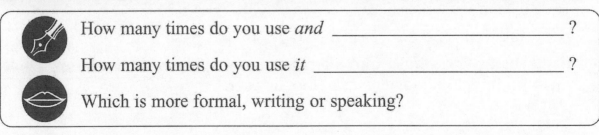

How many times do you use *and* _____ ?

How many times do you use *it* _____ ?

Which is more formal, writing or speaking?

Language Exercises

The verbs **be / have / have got** are important for describing people:

   She **is** small and slim
   She **has** freckles
   He **has got** blonde hair

Have and **Have got** mean the same thing.

1   **Find and highlight all the examples of** *be, have* **and** *have got* **in texts 1 and 2.**

2   **Read the table and discuss the way** *be have* **and** *have got* **are used for describing people:**

Be	age	she	is	10 years old
		he	is in his	twenties
		they	are	in their thirties
	build	she	is	small
		she	is	small <u>and</u> slim
		she	is	small <u>and</u> slim <u>with</u> red hair
		he	is of	medium height
		he	is of	average weight
	personality	she	is	active
		she	is	bright <u>and</u> creative
		he	is	very friendly
Have/Have got	appearance	she	has	freckles
		she	has got	freckles
		he	has	blonde hair <u>with</u> blue eyes
		he	has got	blonde hair <u>with</u> blue eyes
		They	have got	black hair

3   **What other verbs do the writers use to describe Emma and Victor?**
   Find them in the text and make a list of them *eg argues*

Language Exercises continued

4   Fill in the blanks with either *be* or *have* or *have got*:

eg He *is* young with blue eyes.

4a   She _____ a big nose.

4b   They _____ tall and slim.

4c   I _____ in my fifties.

4d   He _____ of average height.

4e   She _____ short, brown hair.

5   Choose the correct word in these sentences

eg   John is ~~in~~ / of medium build.

5a   She is short and / with plump.

5b   They are with / in their teens.

5c   She has got blue eyes and / of long hair.

5d   He is an old man in / with a kind face.

5e   I am dark, in / of my twenties, with / and brown eyes.

6   6a   Work with a partner. Say 5 sentences describing each other.

6b   Write the sentences down and then check each other's work.

7   Find all the adjectives in texts 1 and 2 and highlight them.

eg   Emma is very <u>active</u>.

8   Fill in the table, giving the opposite adjective:

	Adjective	Opposite Adjective
eg	*active*	*inactive*
	small	
	slim	
	bright	
	creative	
	stubborn	
	quiet	
	helpful	
	comfortable	
	friendly	

Writing Exercises

A good description of a person needs:
- to be written in paragraphs
- to have an introduction, a middle and a conclusion
- to have a good first sentence which introduces the person
- to give information about the person
- to show the writer's feelings about the person

① **Work with a partner or alone. Plan a description of a person you like.**

1a First, choose the person and decide what information you want to give.

name_____

how do you know the person? _____

what about the person's age, appearance, personality, interests, occupation, behaviour or any other things?_____

_____

how do you feel about the person? _____

1b Next, make a plan and decide on the order for your ideas. Make notes.

title _____

introduction _____

_____

middle _____

_____

conclusion _____

_____

② **Write the description.**

2a Use the frame on the next page.

2b **Now,** read the description again. Are you happy with it ?
Add or change anything that you think will improve it.
Check: spelling, verbs *be* and *have,* prepositions, adjectives, capital letters and full stops.

2c **Lastly,** write a final draft.

③ **Follow-up**

Write about a person you admire or a person you do not like.

Writing Frame

_____

I would like to describe _____

_____ is _____

_____

_____ has got _____ with _____

_____ and _____

_____

_____ likes _____ and _____

_____

_____

_____

We _____

I hope that _____

_____

Describing People

Text 1 My Sister Ana

1 I thought of writing something about my sister Ana, who is 6 years older than me. We grew up in a close-knit family in a farm in Portugal. Ana was the eldest of 5 children and looked after all of us when the adults were busy in the fields. When we were children we did not play together much, as she seemed so much older than me and I

5 was too busy scaring the chickens or playing with the others. Since then, we have both moved to the city and have families of our own and so I have got to know her much better. She is a woman that I admire and respect.

Ana is small and dark, a typical Portuguese woman. There is nothing very remarkable about her appearance except for her large, expressive eyes. She has short, curly hair

10 which she wears loose. She is of average build and is in her early fifties but looks younger when she smiles. She has got an open, honest face and she laughs all the time. When I think of her, I picture her laughing loudly, rocking her head from side to side. She is an extremely energetic and hard-working woman who is good at most things – cooking, looking after children, listening to others and making a small purse go a long

15 way. Her family adore her. Another characteristic she has is that she is very sociable, her house is always full of friends, relatives and neighbours who drop in for a chat. The thing I like most about her is her realism. If I have a problem, I know that I can discuss it with her and that her advice will always be practical and down to earth. Above all, she will not judge me. She is the sort of person you can trust.

20 They say that blood is thicker than water and in Ana's case that is certainly true. I am very lucky to have her as a sister and as a friend.

Text 2: Dany

1 Dany is like a brother to me. He is in his mid-twenties but appears much older. He has a moustache and a dark, brown beard covering his face. He looks like a pirate, rough and impulsive. Some people would not find him attractive but he is to me.

Although he looks like a bear, healthy and strong, he does not have a bear's grumpy
5 manners.

Sometimes, he forgets how strong he is and occasionally he hurts me. Despite that, he is an easy-going person. He loves helping people by giving his best.

Dany is the only person I know who seems to have no problems. There is an aura of peace, calm and joy that reflects on me and on every person he knows. He is a patient
10 person who knows how to listen to other people's problems. I cannot imagine him ever having any enemies. His eyes reflect his cleverness. He has the happiest personality of all my friends and he is always acting the clown.

People are attracted by this mixture of force and kindness. Physically and mentally, he is a contradiction. Those who pass him in the street and glance at him are often afraid
15 because of his wild look.

Dany does not give a damn about fashion. He always wears jeans, a shirt or pullover if he finds one in his size. When he goes to parties, he hates wearing a suit and tie.

Dany has chosen a good way of life: learn, teach and have fun. He is the most balanced person I know: faithful, reliable, optimistic and generous. He is a miracle in himself.

Reading Exercises

1   Read the titles and the first sentence of each text. Do you think the writers are going to say good or bad things about these people?

2   Read the topic sentences quickly and see if you were right.

3   Read the texts carefully, highlight any words you do not know and look them up in a dictionary or ask your teacher.

Text Analysis

Work with a partner.

1   Find and mark the introduction, middle and conclusion in texts 1 and 2.

2   Discuss the meaning of these words with your teacher or look them up in a dictionary:

appearance	looks	character	personality
behaviour	occupation	interests	relationships

3   **Discuss how the texts are the same or different. Make notes about texts 1 and 2.**

3a   How does the first sentence in each text link to the title?

3b   Read the introduction to each text. Is it a good introduction? Why?

3c   List, in order, the things the writer chooses to say about each person.
Choose from the words in 2.

3d   How does each text finish? Is it a good conclusion? Why?

3e   What are the main tenses used? Why are other tenses sometimes used in the introduction and conclusion?

3f   What purpose did the writers have when they planned their description? What did the writers want you to think about the person they describe?

4   **Describe someone you know well to your partner. Which is more formal, writing or speaking? Think about:**

the use of *and*

the use of *he* or *she*

do you use full sentences when you speak?

are there any words and phrases in the texts you would not use in speech? List three.

How would you say these phrases?

eg   Another characteristic she has is that she is very sociable. (written)
She's very sociable as well. (spoken)

4a   In Text 2, can you find a sentence which is more commonly used in speech? Why has the writer chosen to use it?

Language Exercises

1 **Read and discuss the language used to describe people's age and physical appearance, using the verbs** <u>be</u>   <u>have / have got</u>**:**

be + in **age**	I You He She We	am are is is are	in in in in in	my your his her our	early mid late	teens twenties thirties forties fifties
be + about **age**	They She	are is	about about			sixty twenty-five
be + adjective + with + and **age + features**	I She	am is	middle-aged elderly	with with	curly hair a long face	and dark eyes and glasses
be + of **build**	I He They	am is are	of of of	average medium		height build weight
have or have got **features**	I have I've got He has He's got		blue eyes dark hair a fair complexion fair hair		and and	short, curly hair a bushy beard

2 **Fill in the blanks with language from the table:**

eg He *is* in *his early* sixties.

2a She _____ middle-aged _____ dark eyes _____ grey hair.

2b My children _____ _____ medium build _____ _____ average height.

2c They are tall _____ slim and are _____ thirty.

2d I _____ dark, brown eyes.

3 **Read these 2 sentences from text 1 and 2:**

She is a hardworking woman *who* is good at most things
She has short, curly hair *which* she wears loose
He is a person *who* knows how to listen

3a Re-order these sentences:

eg   me is brother Dany a like to
      Dany is like a brother to me

i.   wears has reading which glasses she for she

ii   house chat her for full a who is drop people in of

iii   football Sam likes man playing is who a

iv   ponytail she red has which long wears hair she a in

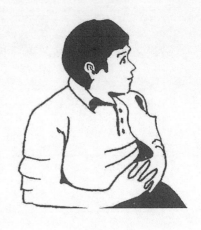

Language Exercises continued

4 **Make sentences describing people using the words given:**

eg middle aged/ very handsome/dark eyes
     He is middle aged and very handsome with dark eyes.

4a Mohammed / in his twenties / moustache /beard

4b Linda / long black hair / in a ponytail

4c a dark complexion / about thirty five / glasses

4d My son / of average height / long, curly, brown hair / loose

4e Ayam / a long nose / a gentle expression

5 **5a To describe a person's personality, the writers use different verbs and adjectives:**

VERBS	ADJECTIVES
eg she laughs _____	*she has an open, honest face*
_____	_____
_____	_____
_____	_____

5a Find and list other verbs and adjectives from texts 1 and 2 which are expressive and interesting.

5c Make your own sentences with them.

eg   is good at...... My son is good at swimming and cycling.

6 **Read these sentences and phrases from Text 2 and find them in the text. Put them under the right headings.**

Another characteristic she has is

When I think of her I

The thing I like most about her is

I thought of writing something about

I hope that

She is the sort of person who

I am very lucky to have her as a sister

Introduction	Information about the person	Conclusion
	eg Another characteristic she has is	

Writing Exercises

A good description of a person needs:

- to be written in paragraphs
- to have an introduction, a middle and a conclusion
- to have a good first sentence which introduces the person
- to give information about the person
- to show the writer's feelings about the person

(1) **Work with a partner or alone. Plan a description of a person you know and like. Use your own language to plan if you prefer.**

1a First, choose the person and decide what information you want to give. Use the mind map below:

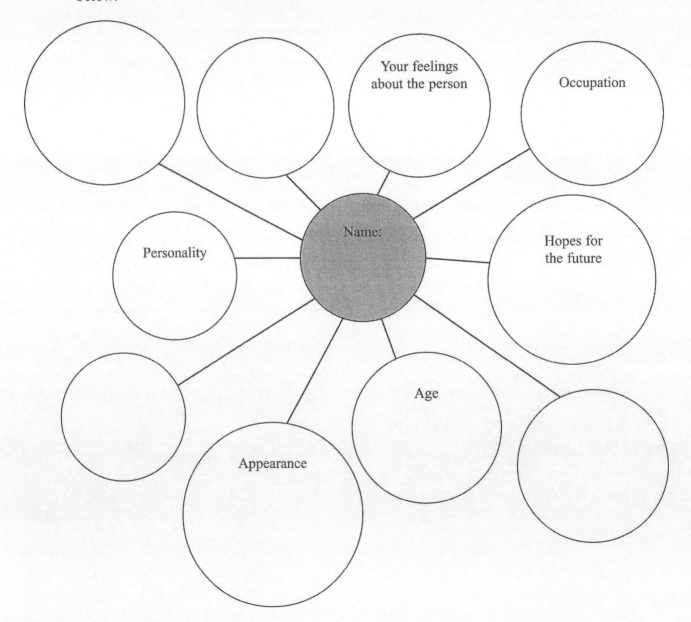

Writing Exercises continued

1b Next, make a written plan and decide on the order for your ideas:

title _____

introduction _____

_____

_____

middle_____

_____

_____

conclusion_____

_____

② **Write the first draft of the description.**

2a Use the frame on the next page to help you.

2b Now read the description again. Are you happy with it? Add or change anything that you think will improve it. **Check:** spelling, verbs *be* and *have,* prepositions, adjectives, capital letters and full stops

③ **Work with a partner and read each other's work.**

3a What do you think the writer feels about the person and why?

3b Is there anything that you do not understand?

3c Check it for the things in 2b. Remember it is always easier to find other people's mistakes than your own.

④ **Lastly,** write a final draft.

⑤ **Follow-up**

Write about a person you admire or a person you do not like.

Writing Frame

_____

I thought of writing something about _____

who is _____

_____

_____

_____ is _____

_____

_____ has got _____ with _____

_____ and _____

_____

When I think of _____ I picture _____

Another characteristic _____ has is _____

_____

Above all _____

We _____

_____

I hope _____

Narratives

Text 1: A Very Wet Day

1 Yesterday I left my house to come to college. It was pouring with rain. I got very wet because I did not have an umbrella. It was a terrible day.

When I arrived at college, I asked my teacher to help me. She gave me some clothes from the store room but they were too big for me. Then, when I walked
5 into the class all the students laughed at me because I was wearing very big clothes!

So, no more outings without an umbrella. I decided to go and buy an umbrella the next day.

Text 2: The Robbery

1 Mrs Brown went to the newsagents last Friday. She did this every Friday. She paid her newspaper bill. It was midday. The sun was shining and it was not cold. It was a perfectly ordinary day.

While Mrs Brown was standing in the shop, the door suddenly opened. A man
5 came in. He was wearing a black mask and he was carrying a gun. He shouted,

"Stay still! Don't move! Give me the money!"

Mrs Brown froze and put her hands up. Then, the robber took the money from the till and ran out. It was all over in seconds. The shop assistant dialled 999.

The police arrived a few minutes later but it was too late. The man had escaped.
10 It was the most frightening experience of Mrs Brown's life.

Reading Exercises

1 Read the stories and underline any words you do not know. Look them up in a dictionary or ask your teacher.

2 Do the stories describe a happy event, a funny event, a frightening event or an embarrassing event?

3 Can you think of a funny, embarrassing or frightening story? Did it happen to you or someone else?

Text Analysis

Narratives are usually stories which happened in the past.
Work with a partner.

1   1a **Find the beginning, middle and end in texts 1 and 2.**

     1b **Read Text 1 again and answer the questions:**

         i)   Who are the characters?

         ii)   Where did the story happen?

         iii) When did it happen?

     1c **Now read Text 2 again and answer the same questions.**

2   **Put these sentences in the order that they happened in the story.**

Text 1	Text 2
When I arrived at college	The police arrived.
All the students laughed at me	Mrs Brown went to the newsagents.
I got very wet	A man came into the shop.
She gave me some clothes	The robber took the money from the till.
Yesterday I left my house	She paid her newspaper bill.
I decided to buy an umbrella	Mrs Brown froze.
It was pouring with rain	He was carrying a gun.
The clothes were very big	The shop assistant dialled 999.
I asked my teacher to help me	He shouted "Stay still! Don't move! Give me the money!"

3   **Find the last sentence in text 1 and 2. Is it a good last sentence? Why? Think of other ways of ending these narratives.**

4   **Think of a funny, frightening or embarrassing story and tell it to your partner. Think about the difference between *telling* and *writing* a story.**

  How many times do you use *and*_____ ?

  How many times do you use *he/she/it* _____ ?

        Which is more formal, writing or speaking?

Language Exercises

1 **1a Find all the words and phrases about time in both texts.**

Text 1 _____   _____

Text 2 _____   _____

1b Why are they important?

2 **2a Read these sentences from Text 2:**

Mrs Brown went to the newsagents last Friday.
She did this every Friday. She paid her bill.
It was midday.

Find all the verbs.
What tense are they in?
Why does the writer use this tense?

2b Fill in the tables using the correct form of the Simple Past.

present simple	past simple
arrive	*eg arrived*
walk	
laugh	
help	
ask	
shout	
move	

present simple	past simple
do	*eg did*
am/is/are	
buy	
find	
come	
go	
take	

2c Read and choose the correct form of the verb.

eg Last week I ~~see~~ / saw my sister.

Yesterday I leave/left my house to come to college. It were/was pouring with

rain. I got/get very wet because I do not/did not have an umbrella. It was/is

very wet. When I arrived/arrive at college, I ask/asked my teacher to help

me. She gave/give me some clothes.

Language Exercises

3 **3a** **Read these sentences:**

When I walked in the students laughed because <u>I was wearing</u> very big clothes.

While Mrs Brown <u>was standing</u> in the shop the door suddenly opened.

3b **What is the name of this tense? Why does the writer use it?**

3c **Is there a tense like this in your language?**

3d **Discuss the difference between the Simple Past and the Past Continuous tenses. Fill in the tables using the correct form of the Past Continuous and Simple Past.**

Present Simple	Past Simple	Past Continuous
I look you look he look**s** she look**s** it look**s** we look you look they look	*eg I looked*	*eg I was looking*

3e **Fill in the missing verbs. Use the verbs in the box. Think carefully about which tense to use.**

While Mrs Brown ¹*was paying her bill* in the shop, the door suddenly

² _____ . A man ³ _____ in. He ⁴ _____ a black

mask and he ⁵ _____ a gun. He ⁶ _____,

"⁷ _____ still! Don't ⁸ _____ ! ⁹ _____ me the money!"

Mrs Brown ¹⁰ _____ and ¹¹ _____ her hands up. Then the

robber ¹² _____ the money from the till and ¹³ _____ out.

It ¹⁴ _____ all over in seconds. The shop assistant ¹⁵ _____ 999.

> be   wear   shout   ~~pay~~   move   put   give
> have   freeze   take   walk   run   dial   open   stay

Writing Exercises

A good narrative needs:
- to be written in paragraphs
- to have a beginning, a middle and an end
- to say what happened and in the right order

① **Work with a partner. Look at the picture story on the next page.**

1a First, tell each other the story.

1b Next, write a plan.
Think about:
Who are the people? Give them names.
Where are they?
When is it?
What happened?

1c Next, decide on the order for your ideas. Make notes:

title   *Parents and Children*

beginning: _____

_____

middle: _____

_____

end: _____

_____

② **Write your narrative.**

2a Use the frame on the next page.

2b Now, read the description again. Are you happy with it ?
Add or change anything that you think will improve it.
Check: spelling, tenses, time words and phrases, capital letters
and full stops.

2c Lastly, write a final draft.

③ **Follow up.** Write a funny or frightening story.

Parents and Children

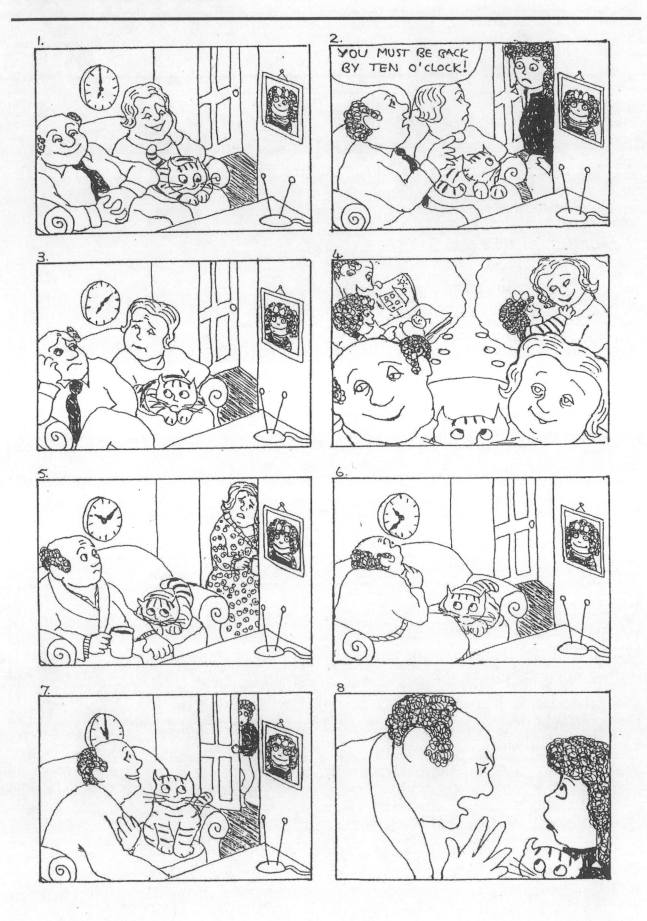

Hazel Hirshorn

Writing Frame

Parents and Children

It was a peaceful Saturday night and while _____

_____

_____

_____

Suddenly, their daughter _____

_____

_____

After she left _____

_____

_____

At ten past ten _____

_____

_____

At last the door opened _____

_____

_____

Narratives

Text 1: The Dead Hen

1 My mother used to keep hens. They were her insurance against bad times, hens being a good source of supply for eggs both to eat and sell, and of meat when they became too old to sell.

One of my most vivid childhood memories concerns a dead hen. What it died of I do
5 not know but I do know my father did not kill it, otherwise we would have eaten it. I grew up after the War. My mother would never waste food.

It was summer. Hot, sultry days changed suddenly to heavy rain. My father could not bury the dead bird straight away because the ground was too wet for digging. He hung it by its tied feet in the coal shed and there it stayed for a week. Now, you are pulling
10 a face imagining its condition, and indeed that is exactly how my mother felt about it. She kept reminding him about the dead hen and finally persuaded him to bury it the following weekend.

Sunday was dry and hot and my father dug a hole at the bottom of the garden. Seeing me standing idly by, he asked if I would fetch the hen. I ran eagerly feeling the
15 importance of being asked to do an unusual job.

I climbed onto the coal and unhooked the bird, admiring once again its beautiful black feathers. What a shame to have to bury it. Poor Elizabeth. I made pets of all of them and they all had names. My sadness turned to excitement as I felt the warmth of her body and saw the movement. Surely my father was mistaken, it was alive! Dead birds
20 went stiff and cold – this was alive and breathing.

I ran back with it to my father, breathless with my news. He was leaning on his spade talking to a neighbour and motioned to me to lay it in the hole. I did not. I stood holding the live bird, crooning to it in my childish way. I looked at the eyes and gently touched one to make her wake up. A maggot fell out. I dropped the loathsome thing and ran
25 screaming to my mother.

I have never been able to eat chicken since or look at a maggot.

Text 2: The Jacket

1   My cousin Jane has a Spanish friend called Claudia who came to visit her last summer. She stayed with Jane for 3 days and then she went back to her flat in Barcelona. That same week, after Claudia left, other friends came to see Jane. They were an older couple called Ken and Lettie. They stayed until Saturday. It was a busy week.

5   That Sunday, as Jane was cleaning the house, she found a lady's jacket. It was black and very new. She was sure that it was Claudia's jacket, so the next day she rushed to the Post Office and sent it to Barcelona. She was very pleased with herself. That evening she boasted to her husband Andrew, saying how organised and efficient she
10 had been.

A few days later the telephone rang and Andrew answered it. He spoke for a few minutes. His eyes were laughing. He hung up and said,

"That was Lettie. She said she thinks she left her black jacket here. She needs it urgently. Her false teeth are in the pocket!"

Reading Exercises

1   Read the stories and underline any words you do not know. Look them up in a dictionary or ask your teacher.

2   Do the stories describe a happy event, a funny event, a frightening event or an embarrassing event?

3   Answer these questions. Circle True or False:

Text 2 is about a frightening event.	True/False
Text 2 took place last summer.	True/False
Text 1 deals with a childhood experience.	True/False
In Text 1 Elizabeth is the narrator.	True/False

4   4a **In Text 2,** how did Andrew feel when he had spoken to Lettie?

4b **In Text 1,** why did the mother remind her husband to bury the bird?

5   5a What is a *"punch line"?*

5b What are the punch lines in texts 1 and 2?

Text Analysis

1 Narratives are often stories which describe a *sequence of events* in the past. They are organised in different ways by different writers It depends on the *writer's purpose.* However, they usually contain *4 elements: characters, setting, events, outcome.*

Match the 4 elements to definitions:

1	characters	a	what happened in the end
2	setting	b	the people or animals that play an important part in the story
3	events	c	the time and place of the story
4	outcome	d	the things that happened

2 **Work with a partner. Complete this table for texts 1 and 2.** Discuss your ideas and then write short notes in the boxes, giving information from the texts:

Characters
Text 1: *eg. the mother*
Text 2:
Setting
Text 1:
Text 2:
Events
Text 1:
Text 2:
Outcome
Text 1:
Text 2:

3 **In text 2, the writer uses irony. What is irony?** Use a dictionary to help you define it. Which part of the story is ironic?

4 **Writers sometimes choose to write in the 1st person ("I...") or in the 3rd person ("He../She..") Who is the narrator in Text 1 and in Text 2?**

5 **Think of a funny, frightening or embarrassing story and tell it to your partner.** Which is more formal, writing or speaking? Think about:

the way you begin and end the narrative

how often you use ....and.... and pronouns, eg he, she

are there words and phrases in Text 1 you would not use in speech?

eg "Seeing me standing idly by..." line 13/14

How would you say this?

Can you find two other examples?

Language Exercises

1   **1a Find the time words and phrases in text 2 and circle them. Some tell you *when* something happened, others tell you *how long for* and others tell you *in what order* things happened.**

   1b Look at the position of these time words and phrases in the sentence. Some are at the beginning and others are in the middle or the end.

   1c Fill in the table using time words and phrases from text 2.

TIME WORDS AND PHRASES	POSITION IN SENTENCE
when	
eg. last summer	*end*
how long for	
order of events	

   1d Re-order the words to make correct sentences.

   Some sentences have more than one possibility.

   i)   I Sunday to am next sister see my going

   ii)   months seen for not two I have months her

   iii) for without I hours yesterday break twelve worked a

   iv)   mother wrote a to Anna her later days few

Language Exercises

2   In narratives the **order or sequence** of events is very important.

   2a Find the following sequencing words in Texts 1 and 2 and underline them. You have already found some of them in Text 2:

   and then   after   as   so   and finally

   _____

   _____

   2b Think of other sequencing words and phrases you can use in a narrative and add them to the list above.

   2c Fill in the gaps in these sentences using one of the sequencing words or phrases you have listed:

   eg   *Finally we arrived home exhausted and went to bed.*

   i   I was late _____ I hurried out of the house _____ jumped on a bus.

   ii   _____ she had breakfast she went to College.

   iii   Yesterday _____ Tom was playing football he fell.

   iv   We went shopping in the morning _____ had a cup of coffee.

   v   They waited all day by the telephone. _____ he rang.

3   Narratives can be more interesting when the writer uses adjectives to create an atmosphere – eg words that describe feelings, sounds, colours, smells.

   3a Find adjectives in each paragraph of text 1 and list them.

   3b Use a thesaurus and find other adjectives with the same meaning and substitute them in the text.

   eg paragraph 1.   *They were her insurance against <u>bad</u> times.*

                               difficult

   3c. Make sentences using the following adjectives:

   vivid, sultry, unusual, stiff, loathsome

4   **Look at this section from Text 1, paragraph 3:**

   My father could not bury the dead bird straightaway because the ground was too wet for digging. He hung it by its tied feet in the coalshed and there it stayed for a week.

   We use words like: **he, it, there** to refer back to things already mentioned in the text. We often use pronouns to do this.

4   **4a Find the pronouns that refer back to things and people in paragraphs 4 and 5 of text 1. Link them with arrows as shown in the example above.**

Writing Exercises

A good narrative usually

* has a beginning, a middle and an end
* is written in paragraphs
* has characters, a setting, a sequence of events and an outcome
* tells a story

The writer of a narrative will have a purpose, for instance, to make the reader laugh or shiver.

① **Work with a partner. Look at the picture story on the next page. Tell the story aloud to each other.**

1a Plan the story. Think about:
* the characters
* the setting
* the sequence of events
* the outcome
* is this a 1st person or 3rd person narrative?

1b Make a written plan:

title	*Upstairs...Downstairs*
beginning	_____
	_____
middle	_____
	_____
end	_____
	_____

② **2a Write the first draft of your narrative.** Use the frame on the next page to help you.

2b Now read your story again. Are you happy with it? Add or change anything that will improve it. **Check:** spelling, tenses, time words and phrases, sequencing words, adjectives, pronouns.

③ **Work with a partner and read each other's work.**

3a Is your partner's version of the story the same as yours?

3b Is there anything that you do not understand?

3c Check it for the things in 2b. Remember it is always easier to find other people's mistakes than your own.

④ **Lastly,** write a final draft of your story.

⑤ **Follow up.**

Write a funny or frightening narrative.

Upstairs Downstairs

Afternoon:

Evening:

Next Day:

or:

or:

Hazel Hirshorn

Writing Frame

Upstairs Downstairs

Yesterday afternoon _____

_____

_____

Downstairs _____

_____

_____

Their mother _____

_____

Later that _____

_____

_____

_____

At the same time _____

_____

The next day _____

_____

_____

Folk Tales

Text 1: Nasruddin's Donkey

1 One day, in an Arabian city, the Mullah Nasruddin was in his garden.
A neighbour came and said to him,
"My dear neighbour, can I borrow your donkey?"

Nasruddin replied,

5 "I am sorry, my donkey is not here. I cannot help you."
Just then, Nasruddin's donkey brayed loudly from its stable at the back of the
house. The neighbour looked at Nasruddin in surprise and said,
"Your donkey is here! Why are you lying to me?"

Nasruddin answered,

10 "My dear friend, who do you believe? Me or my donkey ?"

Text 2: An Indian Tale

1 Once upon a time, a woman went to the market in Maharastra and bought
a beautiful, white goose. You can imagine her surprise later when the goose laid
a silver egg. Each morning for a week, the goose laid a shiny, silver egg.

The woman said,

5 "I will give this goose a lot of food to eat. Maybe it will lay two eggs everyday
and I will become rich. I will live in a big house with many servants and have
expensive clothes and jewels."

So, the woman bought a lot of food for the goose and fed it in the morning, in
the afternoon and in the evening. Sadly, the goose died of over-eating and did not
10 lay any more eggs ever again.

Reading Exercises

1 **Read text 1 and answer these questions:**
   1a Who was Nasruddin?
   1b Where was he?
   1c What did his neighbour want?
   1d Where was the donkey?
   1e Why do you think Nasruddin lied?

2 **Read text 2 and answer these questions:**
   2a Where did the woman live ?
   2b Where did she go and what did she buy?
   2c Why was the goose special ?
   2d What happened to the goose?

3 **Do you know any folk stories from your country?**

Text Analysis

1 **1a Do folk stories have a purpose?**

   1b Put a tick in the box of the table if you agree:

	Nasruddin's Donkey	**An Indian Tale**
Makes you cry Makes you laugh Teaches about God Teaches right from wrong Makes you frightened Makes you think Teaches about society		

   1c Discuss your ideas.

2 **2a Work with a partner. Find the beginning, the middle and the end of text 1 and text 2.**

   2b Read the table and discuss your ideas. Then, fill in the boxes.

Who are the characters?
Text 1:
Text 2:
Where did the story happen?
Text 1:
Text 2:
How does it begin? Is it a common beginning for a folk story?
Text 1:
Text 2:
How does it end? Is it a strong ending? Is this important?
Text 1:
Text 2:
Is the story in the present, the past or the future?
Text 1:
Text 2:

Language Exercises

1 1a Folk stories often begin and end in a special way:

               begin   **end**

       Once upon a time   *...ever again.*

_____   _____

_____   _____

_____   _____

Does this happen in your language?

1b Can you think of other ways of beginning and ending folk tales in English? Add them to the list above.

2 2a Look at these examples of the Past Simple from text 1:

    A neighbour **came** and   **asked** him....
        irregular   *regular*

2b Find all the verbs in the Past Simple in Texts 1 and 2 and list them:

Irregular	Regular
eg *came*	*asked*

2c Fill in the gaps, using a verb from those listed above:

eg The neighbour <u>looked</u> at Nasruddin in surprise.

i) Once upon a time a woman _____ to a market in Maharastra and _____ a goose.

ii) One day the Mullah Nasruddin _____ in his garden.

iii) Each day the goose _____ a silver egg.

iv) The woman _____ the goose every morning, afternoon and evening but it _____

v) A neighbour _____ to Nasruddin's house and _____ if he could borrow his donkey.

Language Exercises continued

3 3a Look at the punctuation for *direct speech* in text 1:

New line
for speech.
Open
speech
marks.

Nasruddin replied,

"I am sorry, my donkey is not here.

I cannot help you."

Comma before
opening speech
marks.

Full stop inside
the closing speech marks.

3b Read this text and re-write it, using the correct punctuation for the direct speech. Check with the example in 3a.

One day, I went to Tom's house. He opened the door and said to me hello, how are you? What are you doing here? I replied I came to see you. He looked very happy and said come in. I'll make us some coffee. I went in and sat down. Tom asked me would you like milk and sugar. I said only milk, thanks.

4 4a These verbs are often used with direct speech. They are in the Simple Past:

said   answered   replied   told   asked

4b Finish these questions and answers using one of the 5 verbs above:

eg *"Can I borrow your donkey?" <u>asked</u> the neighbour.*

i   " What's your name ?" _____ Peter.

ii   " Mr Brown," _____ Mr Brown.

iii   " Please, take a seat," Peter _____.

iv   "Thanks, I've been standing for hours," he _____.

v   Mr Brown _____ Peter the time and he

_____, "It's 5 o'clock."

Writing Exercises

A good folk story :
- is written in paragraphs
- has a beginning, a middle and an end
- often uses a traditional beginning and end
- has a purpose, for instance, to make you laugh, to teach right from wrong

① **Work with a partner. Look at the picture folk story on the next page.**

First, tell each other the story.

1a Then, plan the story. Think about:
- a traditional beginning
- the animals
- where are they?
- what happened?
- a strong end

1b Next, make a plan and decide on the order of your ideas. Make notes.

title	*The Hare and the Tortoise*
beginning	_____
	_____
middle	_____
	_____
	_____
end	_____
	_____

② **Write the story.**

2a Use the frame on the next page.

2b Now read your story again. Are you happy with it?

Add or change anything that will improve it.

Check: spelling, tenses, punctuation, direct speech.

2c Lastly, write a final draft.

③ **Follow-up**

Write a folk story from your country.

The Hare and the Tortoise

Writing Frame

The Hare and the Tortoise

Once upon a time _____

_____

_____

The hare said _____

The tortoise answered _____

So _____

_____

After a while, the hare _____

_____

but the tortoise _____

_____

Much later _____

_____

The tortoise said _____

Folk Tales

Text 1: Shahrezad

1 Once upon a time, in Persia, there lived a powerful and cruel king called Shahriyar. Every evening he chose a young woman from his kingdom to be his bride. However, the following morning, he ordered the new queen to be executed.

One day came the turn of Shahrezad who was as clever as she was beautiful. She was
5 determined to outwit the king.

The night of her marriage, she began to tell Shahriyar a tale. At first, the king listened with little interest but slowly the story caught his imagination. By the morning the tale was unfinished and the king was so intrigued to know the end that he waved away the executioner. Shahriyar asked Shahrezad to continue that evening, which she did. As
10 soon as she had finished the first story, the queen began a second tale which seemed to grow out of the first. This tale was even more interesting than the first but it too was unfinished in the morning. The executioner was sent away a second time.

One story followed another, one day followed another and so it went on for a thousand and one nights. The king fell in love with the lovely story-teller and never called for
15 the executioner again. Shahriyar and Shahrezad lived happily ever after.

Reading Exercises

1   Quickly read the first and last sentence of each paragraph. Have you got the gist (general) meaning of the story?

2.   Read the text carefully and look up any words you do not know or ask your teacher.

3.   What is the moral of the tale?

4.   Do you know any folk stories from your country?

Text 2: The Hen and the Dove (Ashanti Tale, Ghana)

1 Long, long ago, in Africa there were two hungry friends, Akoko, the hen and Aturukuku, the dove. One day Akoko said,

"We must leave this place and look for food. You go to the tall grass country and I will go to the village where men live. If you find food, come and tell me and if I find

5 food, I will come and tell you."

So, Akoko went to a nearby village. While she was searching for seeds and grain, a woman saw her and caught her. She tied the hen by the leg with a strong piece of rope. Akoko did not like the rope but she enjoyed the water and scraps of food that the woman gave her every evening.

10 After some days, Aturukuku found Akoko who asked,

"My friend, did you find any food in the tall grass country?"

Aturukuku replied,

"It is very difficult. I have to scratch and scrape to find any food at all."

"Too bad!" said Akoko, "Look at me. See how fat I am! I am an important person here."

15 The next evening, Aturukuku went back to visit her friend but she was gone. She asked a cat who was lying under a tree,

"Where is Akoko?"

"Oh," he purred, "She was fat and juicy so my mistress put her in the cooking pot."

Aturukuku felt sad and flew away. She said to herself,

20 "My life is hard but at least I am free and can fly away across the sky."

Reading Exercises

1. **Read the text.**

2. **Make notes about the story using the mind map on the following page.**

Mind map

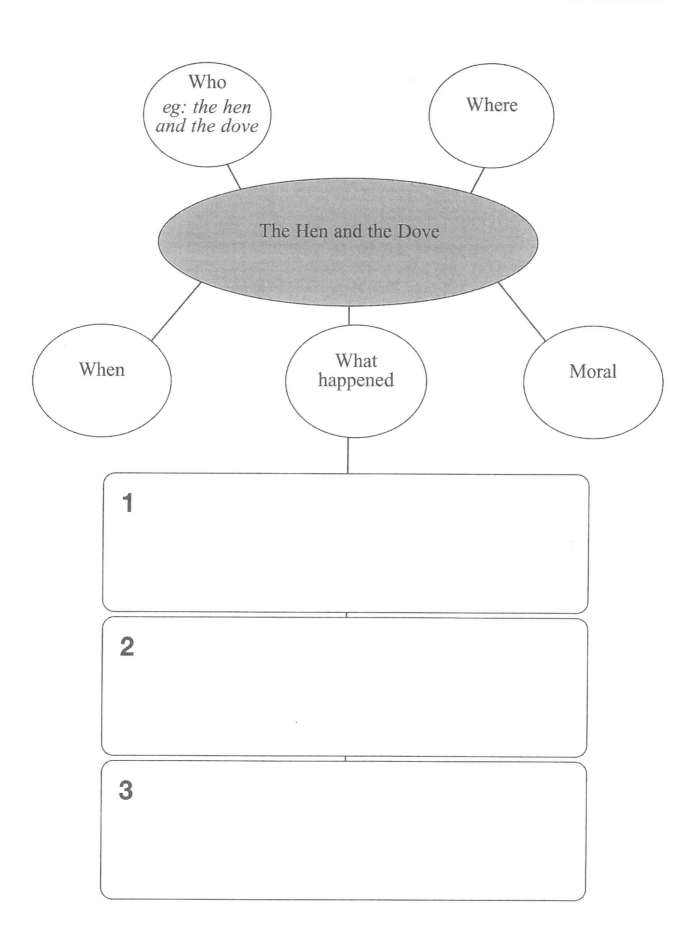

Text Analysis

1 **1a Work with a partner.** Find the introduction, middle and conclusion of texts 1 and 2 and mark them by the margin.

   1b Read these sentences and circle true or false. If you think it is false, what in your opinion is the right answer?

    i   the introduction tells the reader who, where and when   True   False

    ii the middle gives you background information to the action   True   False

    iii the conclusion tells you what happened in chronological order   True   False

    iv the introduction tells you the moral or the story's outcome   True   False

2 **2a** Folk stories in English often begin and end in a traditional way, indicating to the reader that they are reading a folk story. **Find these traditional phrases in texts 1 and 2 and write them below.**

Beginning	Ending

   2b Can you think of others to add to the list?

   2c Is there something similar in your language?

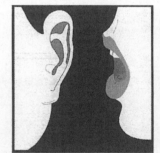

3 **3a What is the main tense used in the narrative in texts 1 and 2?**

   3b Could the story also be told in the present?

   3c Would this make the atmosphere more:
    – serious
    – dramatic
    – exciting
    – moving

   3d What tense or tenses are used in telling folk stories in your language?

Language Exercises

1   1a **Look at the example of direct speech from text 1:**

After some days, Aturukuku found Akoko who asked,
"My friend, did you find any food in the tall grass country?"

Aturukuku replied,
"It is very difficult. I have to scratch and scrape to find any food at all."

1b Look carefully at the punctuation and answer these questions:

i   How does the reader know that these are Akoko and Aturukuku's actual words?

ii   What must the writer put before opening the speech marks?

iii Does the direct speech go on a new line?

iv   Does this happen every time?

1c Work with a partner. Discuss the punctuation rules for direct speech and complete these sentences:

i   A writer uses speech marks when _____

_____

ii   A writer begins a new line _____

_____

iii A writer puts a comma before _____

_____

iv   Each time a different person speaks the writer should open _____

_____

v   Before closing the speech marks the writer _____

_____

2   2a **Read "Nasruddin's Donkey" Text 1, page.**

2b Below is that story without the correct punctuation for the direct speech. **Write the story out again, using the correct punctuation.**

One day, in an Arabian city, the Mullah Nasruddin was in his garden. A neighbour came and said to him my dear neighbour, can I borrow your donkey Nasruddin replied I am sorry, my donkey is not here. I cannot help you. Just then, Nasruddin's donkey brayed loudly from its stable at the back of the house. The neighbour looked at Nasruddin in surprise and said your donkey is here! Why are you lying to me? Nasruddin answered my dear friend, who do you believe? Me or my donkey?

3 Writers often like to join short sentences together to make longer, more complex sentences. There are different ways of doing this. One of them is using **who which where** (relative pronouns).

3a Read these two sentences.

She saw a **man**. The **man** was lying under a tree.

The word **man** is in both sentences. You can join the sentences like this:
She saw a man *who was lying under a tree*.

The part in italics is a relative clause. In the relative clause you replace **the man** by **who**. **Who** is used for a person or people. The relative clause comes immediately after the noun it describes.

3b You can do the same for things:
I made a cake. The cake was for the school fair.
I made a cake **which** was for the school fair.
You replace cake by **which. Which** is used for things.

3c You can do the same for places:
I live in London. There are many people in London.
I live in London **where** there are many people.
You replace London by **where. Where** is used for places <u>when there is a preposition in front of the place</u> (eg in, on, at, to). If there is no preposition in front of the place, you replace it by **which**.

London is a city. London has many cars.
London is a city which has many cars.

4 **Read texts 1 and 2 and underline all the relative clauses. Circle the relative pronouns** *who which where.*

5 **Practice joining these pairs of sentences to make 1 longer sentence, using** *who, which* **or** *where.*

5a i Nelson Mandela is a politician.
ii He was in prison for many years.

5b i He lives in South Africa.
ii He became the first black President of South Africa.

5c i He led the African National Congress.
ii The African National Congress came to power in 1995.

6 **Fill in the gaps, using** *who, which* **or** *where:*

Charles Dickens was an English writer _____ was born in 1812. He

wrote many novels _____ are still read today. Dickens, _____

experienced poverty as a child, wrote many books _____ described the condition

of the poor in Victorian England. He spent much of his life in London _____

he worked as a novelist and reporter.

Writing Exercises

A good folk story usually has a moral and

- is written in paragraphs
- has a beginning, a middle and an end
- often uses a traditional beginning and ending
- introduces the characters and the setting at the beginning
- tells the story in chronological order
- has a strong end

① **Work with a partner. Look at the picture folk story on the next page. Write it together but first:**

1a Plan the story. Use your language to plan, if you prefer. Think about:

a traditional beginning

the characters

where are they?

what happened?

a strong end

1b Make a written plan. Write short notes.

title   *The Man, the Monkey and the Hat*

beginning _____

_____

middle_____

_____

end _____

_____

② **2a Next,** write the first draft of your folk story.

Use the frame on the next page.

2b Now read your folk story again. Are you happy with it?

Add or change anything that will improve it.

Check: spelling, tenses, sentence structure, punctuation, direct speech.

③ **Work with a partner and read each other's work.**

3a Is your partner's version of the story the same as yours?

3b Is there anything that you do not understand?

3c Check it for the things in 2b. Remember it is always easier to find other people's mistakes than your own.

④ **Lastly,** write a final draft of your story.

⑤ **Follow-up** Write a folk story from your country.

The Man, the Monkey and the Hat

Writing Frame

The Man, the Monkey and the Hat

Long, long ago in _____

there was _____ who _____

_____ .

One day _____

_____

After a while _____

_____ However, _____

_____

When _____

_____ but _____

_____

_____

First _____

_____

Then _____

_____

but _____

At last _____

_____

_____

Formal Letters

Letter 1

8 Woodside Road
Kingston

April 23rd

Dear Marina,

I am sorry I can not come to class next Monday because my brother is getting married. The wedding is in Leicester on Sunday but we will not come back until Monday evening.

Please can you give handouts and homework to Amina? She will put them through my letter box on her way home.

See you on Wednesday.

Best wishes,

Halima

(Halima Mohamed)

Letter 2

25 Heaton Park
Bradford 9

January 15th.

Dear Ms Russell,

I am sorry that Louisa could not come to school yesterday because she had a very sore throat.

She is better today but I do not think she is well enough to go swimming. Please can she be excused swimming?

Thank you very much.

Yours sincerely,

Helena Massimo

Helena Massimo (Mrs)

Reading Exercises

1   **Read letters 1 and 2.**

1a Who is each letter for?

1b Why are the writers sending the letters?

1c What do the writers want?

Text Analysis

Work with a partner:

1 Read both letters and fill in the table.

How does the writer start? Letter 1: *eg Dear Marina*
Letter 2:
Write the first 3 words of sentence one. Letter 1:
Letter 2:
Write the last sentence. Letter 1:
Letter 2:
How does the writer end? Letter 1:
Letter 2:

2 Both letters:
  2a say sorry – find this part
  2b say why – find this part
  2c ask for something – find this part.

Would you write these 3 things in the same order in your language? If not, how would you write them?

3 Choose the correct ending:
  3a Letter 1 is about   what happened in the past.
                          what will happen in the future.
  3b Letter 1 is about   what happened in the past.
                          what will happen in the future.

Text Analysis continued

4 **Imagine you are Halima and your partner is Marina.**

4a Role-play the conversation.

4b Discuss the difference between *speaking* and *writing*.
Which is more formal? When speaking, do you say
"I can not come..." *"We will not come back...."*
do we use *can't, won't, didn't* in formal writing?

5 **5a** **Look at the letters and compare them with the letter layouts below.**

5b **Match the numbers on the layouts with the things listed on the right.**

1

2

3

4

5

6

7

Letter 1:

the closing of the letter ☐

the date ☐

the opening of the letter ☐

the sender's printed name ☐

the letter ☐

the sender's address ☐

eg the signature 6

Language Exercises

1   **We use *because* to give an explanation.
    Join the sentences:**

I will be late tomorrow because   I will be on holiday.

I cannot come to your party next week because   he is working on that day.

He will have to change his appointment because   I was very busy last week.

Maria did not come to school last week because   I have to go to the dentist.

I have not done my homework because   she had chicken pox.

2   **Now make your own sentences using *because*.**

   2a Ali cannot come to school tomorrow _____

   _____

   2b Marva did not finish her homework last night _____

   _____

   2c I will have to leave early on Tuesday _____

   _____

   2d I could not phone yesterday _____

   _____

   2e _____

   _____

Language Exercises continued

3   Look at these sentences from the letters. They both use *can/could* which are very useful when giving explanations:

I *cannot* come to class next Monday...

Louisa *could not* come to school yesterday...

3a Which sentence is about the past?
    Which sentence is about the future? How do you know?

3b Are the sentences positive or negative? How do you know?

3c Fill in the table with the following sentences:

    I can come   I cannot come

    I could come   I could not come

	past	present/future
positive	*eg I could come*	
negative		

4   We use can in three ways:

    i   to talk about ability eg *I can speak English.*

    ii   to talk about permission eg *Children of 16 can buy cigarettes.*

    iii to make requests eg *Can you give handouts to Amina?*

5   Find *can* and *could* in the letters. How is the writer using them? With a partner think of 3 sentences using *can* to make a request.

    5a _____

        _____

    5b _____

        _____

    5c _____

        _____

Writing Exercises

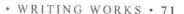

In a letter of explanation you need to:
- start and end the letter correctly
- say why you are writing at the beginning of the letter
- give a reason
- maybe, ask for something.

① **Work with a partner or alone. Write a letter of explanation. You are invited to a friend's wedding but you cannot go.**

   1a First, decide what information you want to give:

   who is the letter for?   why are you saying sorry?

   is it about the past or the future?   what is the explanation?

   do you want anything more?

   1b Next, make a plan. Decide on the order of your ideas. Make notes:

   beginning: _____

   _____

   _____

   middle: _____

   _____

   _____

   end: _____

   _____

   _____

② **Write the letter.**

   2a Use the frame on the next page.

   2b Now, read your letter again. Are you happy with it?

   Add or change anything that will improve it.

   Check: spelling, prepositions, capital letters and full stops, layout.

   2c Lastly, write a final draft.

③ **Follow up**

   Write another letter, changing a hospital appointment.

Writing Frame

(your address) _____

_____

(date) _____

Dear _____

I am sorry _____

_____

because _____

_____

_____

_____

Please can _____

_____

Thank you very much.

_____

_____

_____ (your name)

Formal Letters

Letter 1

35 Buckland Court
Courland Road
London SW12 8GH
13th February 1999

Councillor Timms
Wandsworth Council
Wandsworth Town Hall
London SW11 9PJ.

Dear Councillor Timms,

Crossing in front of Raven School

I am writing to complain about the crossing in front of my son's school. In spite of repeated requests to the Council, there are still no yellow lines on either side of the road, and the cars are still parking right up to the crossing. This is very dangerous because the children cannot see when a car is coming.

The council has promised to put yellow lines on either side of the school gate. Please can you do this as soon as possible, or there will be a terrible accident.

I look forward to hearing from you very soon.

Yours sincerely,

Fatima Masood

Fatima Masood
Chair of the Parent Teacher Association
Raven School.

Letter 2

London Language Centre
St. Mary's Road
Peckham, London SE2 3BN

Your ref: PF/34
22.2.99

The Manager
British Telephones Company
Borough High Street
London SE1 2BN.

Dear Sir,

Re: London Language Centre telephones

Following our telephone conversation this morning, we are writing to confirm that our new telephone system is still not working.

You installed the system last week on the 15th February. However, our customers are still having problems getting through to us. They tell us the phone rings but no-one answers. Although we are all in the office we do not hear it ringing.

Please can you send someone to mend the phones as soon as possible, as we are losing important business.

I look forward to hearing from you and to seeing your engineer in the immediate future.

Yours faithfully,

Kay Drucker

Kay Drucker
Office Manager

Reading Exercises

1   **Look very quickly at the 2 letters:** Who are the letters for? What are the letters about?
2   **Now read the letters fully.** Circle the main complaint. Circle what the writers wants.
3   **Underline the words you do not know.** Ask your teacher or look them up in the dictionary.

Text Analysis

1   **Work with a partner. Compare the two letters. Are they the same or different? Write examples in the table.**

How does the writer start?
Letter 1: *eg Dear Councillor Timms*
Letter 2:
What is the letter about?
Letter 1:
Letter 2:
How is the subject introduced? (eg the first sentence)
Letter 1:
Letter 2:
How does the writer end?
Letter 1:
Letter 2:

2   **What is the purpose of each letter? Where does the writer state it? Would this be the same in your language?**

3   **Look at the order of ideas in each letter. With a partner, answer the questions and make notes:**

   3a Main complaint: What are the main complaints in letters 1 and 2?

   3b Expand the complaint: What is happening in letters 1 and 2?

   3c Request/Demand: What does Fatima Masood want the Council to do and what does Kay Drucker want the telephone company to do?

4   **Imagine you are Fatima Masood and your partner is Councillor Timms. You have a meeting about the problem.**

>   **4a** Role-play the conversation.
>   **4b** Discuss the difference between speaking and writing:
>   • when would you give your name and say you are the Chair of the PTA?
>   • when would you make the main complaint?
>   • which is more formal, speaking or writing?
>   • do we use short forms (eg, *can't isn't*) in formal writing?
>   • when speaking, do we usually say *"I look forward to hearing from you...."* What might you say instead?

Language Exercises

1   **Underline *but, as, because,* or *and* in letters 1 and 2. They are conjunctions. They join two halves of the sentence together.** Insert *but, as, because,* or *and* to join the sentence:

eg This is very dangerous	*as*	the children cannot see when a car is coming
We are all in the office		we do not hear the phone ringing.
There are no yellow lines on either side of the road		the cars park right up to the crossing.
The Council has promised to act		nothing has happened.
Please mend the phones		we are losing important business

2   **2a These are all ways of starting a letter of complaint:**

I am writing to complain about ...   We would like to inform you that ...
We are extremely concerned that ...   We would like to complain about ...
Following our telephone conversation this morning, we are writing to confirm that ...

With a partner, make up six complaints, using all of these starting phrases.
eg the train was 2 hours late; you were given a parking ticket but you have a resident's permit; the refuse collectors did not empty your bin.

2b Look at letters 1 and 2. What phrase do both writers use to ask for something to be done? Use this phrase to ask for action in your six complaints.

2c These are all ways of ending a formal letter: and of showing urgency:

I look forward to   hearing from you   very soon
                    seeing you   in the immediate future
                    meeting you   as soon as possible

3   **Read the letters again.**

3a Has the writer complained before? How do you know? Write the phrases that tell you:

_____

_____

_____

3b Compare these sentences:

Example 1	Example 2
...the cars are still parking right up to the crossing.	...the cars park right up to the crossing.
...our new telephone system is still not working.	...our new telephone system does not work.

Which ones do the writers use in their letters of complaint? What is the difference in meaning between the sentences in example 1 and those in example 2?

What is the name of the tense in example 1? This tense is often used in a letter of complaint to show that something should have changed but has not.

Language Exercises continued

3c Fill in the gaps using the correct form of the verb in brackets.

eg Although we paid our gas bill on the 16th April we *are* *still* *getting* reminders. (get)

    i   Despite several telephone calls we _____ _____ _____ for delivery of the new fridge. (wait)

    ii Although your plumber has been three times, the washing machine _____ _____ _____. (leak)

    iii Even though the Mosque has made repeated requests, the school _____ _____ not _____ halal meat. (serve)

4   4a Look at the letters and compare them with the letter layouts below.

    4b Match the numbers on the layouts with the things listed on the left.

Letter 1:

the closing of the letter ☐

the sender's printed name and title ☐

the date ☐

the opening of the letter ☐

the recipient's address ☐

the letter ☐

eg the sender's address ☐ 1

the signature ☐

Writing Exercises

In a letter of complaint you need to:

- decide on the correct layout
- start and end the letter correctly
- state the complaint
- describe the background to the complaint
- say what you want to happen in the future

① **Work with a partner or alone. Write a letter of complaint to the Council, complaining about the rent increase on the hall your community group hires on Saturdays. Use your own language to plan if you prefer.**

1a First decide what information you want to give:

Who is the letter for?	Who is the letter from?
What is the complaint about?	What is the current situation?
What could happen in the future?	What do you want the Council to do?
How will you start and finish the letter?	How will you lay out the letter?

1b Next, decide on the order for your ideas. Make notes:

beginning _____

_____

middle _____

_____

_____

end _____

_____

② **Write the letter.**

2a Write the first draft, using the frame on the next page to help you.

2b Now, read the draft again. Are you happy with it? Add or change anything that will improve it. **Check:** the order of your ideas and paragraphing, spelling, tense and other grammar, punctuation.

③ **Work with a partner and read each other's work.**

3a What does the writer want to complain about and why?

3b Is there anything that you do not understand?

3c Check it for the things in 2b. Remember it is always easier to find other people's mistakes than your own.

④ **Lastly,** write a final draft.

⑤ **Follow up**

Write a letter of complaint to your local college. They are planning to cut the ESOL classes next year by half.

Writing Frame

Dear

Re:

I am writing to complain about _____

_____

The Council, _____

_____

_____

Please can you _____

_____

I look forward to hearing from you.

Yours _____

_____

Applying for Work

Letter 1

13 Moorfoot Avenue
Sheffield
S13 8BU

23rd February 2001

The Manager
Interpreting Service
Bradford Royal Infirmary
Bradford BD6 7MM

Dear Sir/Madam

Re: Interpreting

I am writing to ask if you have any work for an English/Somali interpreter, paid or unpaid. I enclose my C.V.

As you can see from my C.V., I have the Institute of Linguists Certificate in Community Interpreting from Sheffield College. I have also worked as a volunteer, interpreting for people from my community at the DSS, Housing Department and hospital, since 1996.

I am willing to work in the day or the evening. I look forward to hearing from you.

Yours faithfully,

Amina Ali Mohamed

Amina Ali Mohamed

Letter 2

16 Airdale Avenue
London SW4 8BN

15th March 2001

Selima Ahmed
Nightingale Playgroup
Rectory Road
London SW12 6SD

Dear Ms Ahmed

re: Play Worker

I saw your advertisement for a play worker in the Clapham News this week, and would like to apply. I enclose my C.V.

As you can see from my C.V. I have seven years experience in a nursery school in Colombia, and I have NVQ level 2 in Nursery Nursing from Lambeth College. I have also helped in Clapham After School Centre as a volunteer for 6 months.

I hope you can consider me for the job.

Yours sincerely,

Maria Delgado

Maria Delgado

Reading Exercises

1   **Look very quickly at these letters. What are they about? How do you know?**

2   **Now read them in full and answer the questions.**

   2a Which letter is in answer to an advertisement?

   2b Which writer has experience from her country?

   2c Which writer has worked as a volunteer?

   2d Which writer is willing to work in the evening? Why might this be necessary?

Text Analysis

Work with a partner.

1 **Look at letters 1 and 2 and find the beginning, middle and end.** Match these headings with each paragraph: (i) qualifications and experience, (ii) hopes (iii) reason for writing. In your country would you put the reason for writing at the beginning or at the end?

2 **Compare the two letters and fill in the table. Make short notes.**

How does the writer start?
Letter 1: eg *Dear Sir/Madam*
Letter 2:
What kind of job does the writer want?
Letter 1:
Letter 2:
What qualifications does the writer have?
Letter 1:
Letter 2:
What experience does the writer have?
Letter 1:
Letter 2:
How does the writer end?
Letter 1:
Letter 2:

3 **With a partner, role-play telephoning to ask for a job. Take it in turns to be the employer and the person asking for work.** Look at the difference between asking for work on the phone or in person and writing to ask for work. Would you say or write these phrases? Tick ✔ the right box.

	speaking	writing
eg I look forward to hearing from you.	☐	✔
2a When will you let me know?	☐	☐
2b I enclose my C.V.	☐	☐
2c I'm happy to work evenings.	☐	☐
2d I hope you can consider me for the job.	☐	☐
2e I've been in a nursery on work experience.	☐	☐

Language Exercises

1   Match the word with the definition.

C.V.   things you have done

apply for a job or course   someone who works but does not get paid

experience   send with a letter

eg volunteer   ask someone to give you a job or a place on a
                                   course

enclose   written information about your life, showing your
                                   education and work history, giving dates.

2   Useful language for application letters:

starting	I am writing **to**	ask about		the job the course the vacancy
	I would like to apply **for**	the job **of**		playworker interpreter
	I saw your advertisement **in**	the Job Centre The Clapham News		
	I enclose my	C.V. application form		
describing experience	I have		5 years experience **in**	a school
describing qualifications	I have a	Diploma **in** ... Degree **in** ... Certificate **in** ...	...from	Shipley College Bolivia
finishing	I look forward to hearing from you. I hope you can consider me for the job.			

2a Find some of these in the letters and underline them.

Language Exercises continued

3 Fill the gaps using the words from the box.

eg   I *am writing* to ask about the Playworkers course.

3a I _____ like to _____ for the _____ of cook in your cafe.

3b I _____ your _____ in the Birmingham News and
_____to apply for the _____ of interpreter.

3c I _____ my C.V.

3d I have five years _____ in a nursery.

3e I _____ a Certificate in Interpreting _____ Sheffield College.

3f I _____ _____ to hearing from you.

3g I hope you _____ _____ me for this job.

4 4a Look at these sentences:

I have worked in a nursery school for seven years.

I have worked in a nursery school since 1992.

Discuss with a partner when you use *for* and when you use *since*.

4b Fill the gaps with for or since.

eg   I have been an interpreter *since* 1995.

i) I have worked in a nursery   _____ seven years.

ii) I have helped in the cafe   _____ 1997.

iii)I have studied computing   _____ six months.

iv)I have been a volunteer   _____ a year.

v) I have worked in the garage   _____ January.

Writing Exercises

In a letter of application you need to:
- start and end the letter correctly
- say why you are writing
- give your qualifications and experience

(1) **Work with a partner or alone. Write a letter of application, for a job, for voluntary work or for a course.**

1a First, decide what information you want to give:

what is the job or course?

what qualifications do you have for it?

what useful experience do you have?

1b Next, make a plan. Decide on the order for your ideas. Write short notes:

beginning   _____

             _____

             _____

middle   _____

             _____

end   _____

             _____

             _____

(2) **Write the letter.**

2a Use the frame on the next page.

2b Now, read your letter again. Are you happy with it?

Add or change anything that will improve it.

Check: spelling, prepositions, capital letters and full stops.

2c Lastly, write a final draft.

(3) **Follow up**

Write another letter, replying to an advertisement.

Writing Frame

Applying for work

(your address): _____

_____

(date): _____

_____ (name)

_____

_____

_____ (address)

Dear _____

Re: _____

I am writing _____

_____ I enclose _____

As you can see from my _____ I have _____

_____ from _____ I have also

_____

_____

I hope _____

_____

Yours _____

_____

_____ (your name)

Applying for Courses

Text 1: Supporting statement for an application to a B.Ed course

1 I am applying for a B.Ed course because I was a teacher in Nigeria and I would like to continue that career in this country. I very much enjoyed my six years teaching upper primary children and gained a great deal of satisfaction when I saw the children respond and understand the things I taught. I enjoyed thinking of different ways to
5 arouse the children's interest and create a lively atmosphere for their learning. I also gained satisfaction from the counselling side of the teacher's work and took pleasure in seeing the children develop socially and emotionally.

Now I have my own children whom I teach daily at home; this gives me more practice and experience of teaching, evaluating and monitoring children's development.

10 Following their school career has given me an insight into the differences between education in the United Kingdom and Nigeria, and I am interested in exploring these further through my B.Ed studies.

In Nigeria I studied education with English as my teaching subject. The education aspect entailed psychology and sociology of education, teaching methodology
15 including discipline, teaching practice, teaching resources and the code of conduct expected of a teacher. The English part of the course covered English language, including grammar, and English literature written by English and African authors. My special subject was African writers, and I would enjoy following up this subject in future studies. I write as a hobby and am interested in working with children to
20 encourage them to write both prose and poetry.

Since I came to England five years ago I have worked as a volunteer in a community school in Camberwell on Saturdays, teaching English to children from the ages of 7 to 16. This has given me an insight into the National Curriculum for English, and has shown me the kinds of problems that children have in schools in this country. For
25 instance we have children of 12 and 13 who still have difficulty in reading. This means that they cannot get on with their other subjects, for instance history or geography, as they are not able to read the books and worksheets.

As well as working in the community school, I help out at my Church, both with the Sunday school and with the Choir. These activities bring me into contact with other
30 people and have given me experience of working as a member of a team. This will be useful, both at university and in the teaching practice part of my course.

Text 2: Supporting statement for an application to a Business Studies course

1   I am applying to study for a degree in Business Studies specialising in Management because I particularly enjoyed the Management part of my GNVQ Advanced course and because I worked in management in my country for 3 years before coming to the UK. In that job I was responsible for managing a printing workshop and had a number

5   of management responsibilities; for instance budgeting, personnel, and sales. I was particularly interested in the personnel aspect of the job and look forward to doing more studying in this area.

My work experience in the head office of The Pizza Palace gave me experience of office practice in this country. As part of my work experience I developed a database

10   of regular customers, and I then trained the other staff in how to use it. This showed me how IT skills are used practically in business, and helped me develop my interpersonal skills.

My current GNVQ course has provided me with a wide background to business in this country and in Europe. We studied maths, statistics and accounting as well as

15   personnel, marketing and business law. In my second term we had a week's exchange with a similar course in Germany, and I was able to see how business practice and business studies courses in Germany are both similar and different to those in England.

My GNVQ course and my previous experience have given me a number of skills. I

20   am used to operating in different working cultures. I can speak Arabic and English fluently, and am currently improving my GCSE level German. I have had to develop IT and research skills and am now able to use common software packages and use the internet to find information.

I have also had to develop team-work skills as many of our assignments were done

25   as part of teams. All of this will prepare me for the more rigorous work of the degree course.

Outside my studies and work, I enjoy spending time with my children, and working for my community. I help my community organisation with their accounts and am on the management committee. This has given me experience of how voluntary groups

30   operate.

I feel I have the skills and experience to do a business studies degree. After I finish my studies I would like to work in either personnel or IT management, and a business studies degree will give me the skills for either of these.

Reading Exercises

1   **Look at the titles of both texts. What do you think the writer will say?**

2   **Read both texts and see if you predicted correctly.**

3   **For both texts, make lists of the experience and the skills the writer has.**

Text Analysis

Work with a partner.

1 **Compare both texts and answer the questions.**

1a Is the information the writer must put in the supporting statement different from the information she needs to put in the rest of the form? If so, how?

1b How does the writer start in each text? Is it a good start? Why?

1c How does the writer end in each text? Is it a good ending? Why?

1d Which three tenses are used the most? Give examples of each one. Why does the writer use these tenses?

1e Which paragraph gives information about the following? (Some paragraphs give information about more than one.)
- former studies
- career aspirations
- prior experience
- voluntary work
- why you want to do the course
- outside interests
- current experience

1f Look at the order of the paragraphs? Is this the order that you would use? If not, why not?

1g Look at this sentence *"I am applying for the B.Ed course because I am working as a care assistant at the moment and am finding it boring."* Is this a good sentence to use? Give reasons for your answer.

2 **2a Tell your partner about the skills and experience you have to do a particular job or course.**

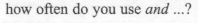

2b Think about how *telling* someone is different from *writing* a statement. Which is more formal, writing or speaking?

how often do you use *and* ...?

how often do you use *it* ...?

do you use full sentences when you speak?

2c Look at the texts again. Are there any phrases in the texts you would not use in speech? List them. How would you say these phrases?

eg I would like to continue that career in this country. (written)
I would like to carry on teaching here. (spoken)

Language Exercises

1   Useful language for applications:

			because I ...	and I would ...
1a	**starting**	I am applying for ... I would like to apply for ...		
1b	**saying why you want to do the course**	I enjoy ... I gain satisfaction from ... I am interested in ... I like/love ... I take pleasure in ... I find ... rewarding		
1c	**saying what you can do**	I can ... I am able to ... I have experience of ... I have had to develop skills in ... I am used to ...		
1d	**saying what you have done and learnt**	I had practice in ... I was responsible for ... This gave me experience of/practice in ... This gave me an insight into ... This has helped me develop ... skills This has shown me how		
1e	**stating your future hopes/plans**	I would like to ... I hope to ... I intend to apply for ...		

2   Find examples of these phrases in the texts and highlight them.

3   Work with a partner. Look at these sentences:

I am interested in *exploring* these differences further.
I am used to *working* as a team member.
I enjoy *teaching*.

I can *use* a number of packages.
I am able to *work* as a team member.
I have had to *develop* IT skills.

3a Discuss how they are different. Now go back to the useful phrases in exercise 1, using the verb *teach*, complete the expressions beginning with 1b. *eg I enjoy teaching*

3   Look at these sentences:

I *work* in a Sunday school. This *gives* me experience of the National Curriculum.

I *worked* as a manager in a printing shop. This *gave* me experience of budgeting.

I *have worked* as a nurse in the emergency department for 2 years. This *has given* me experience of working under pressure.

3a   What is the name of each tense? How does the use of different tenses change the meaning of the sentences?

3b   Find three examples of each tense in texts 1 and 2.

3c   Fill the gaps with the correct tense.

> *eg   I help in the community school every Saturday. (help)*
>
> (i)   I _____ seven year olds when I was in Colombia. (teach)
>
> (ii)   I _____ as an accountant since I left school. (work)
>
> (iii) My experience in Nigeria _____ me how children learn best. (show)
>
> (iv) I _____ computing for the last three years. (study)
>
> (v)   My work is very challenging but I _____ it. (love)
>
> (vi) I work with my children at home, this _____ me great satisfaction. (give)

4   Look at these sentences:

I have a great deal of *practiCe* in accounting.   My careers tutor gave me *adviCe*.

I hope to *practiSe* my French.   I would like to *adviSe* refugees...

Why are the words spelt differently? When do you use practice/advice and when do you use practise/advise? Think of a way to remember which spelling you need to use and when you use it.

5   Fill in the gaps in the following paragraphs:

As part of my work experience I developed a database of regular customers, and I then trained

the other staff in how to use _____. _____ showed me how IT skills

are used practically in business, and helped me develop my interpersonal skills.

As well as working in the community school, I help out at my Church, both with the Sunday

school and with the Choir. _____ activities bring me into contact with other people

and have given me experience of working as a member of a team. _____ will be useful,

both at university and in the teaching practice part of my course.

Writing Exercises

(1) **Work with a partner and discuss:**

1a What should a good application contain?

1b How should it be structured?

(2) **Work with a partner or alone. Plan an application for a course. Use your own language to plan, if you prefer.**

2a First, choose the course and decide what information you need to give:

- why you want to do the course
- relevant work experience, including voluntary work
- relevant studies
- other interests
- the skills that you have developed from all of these that will help you do the course
- plans for the future

2b Next, make a written plan and decide on the order for your ideas. Write short notes.

introduction _____

middle _____

conclusion _____

(3) **3a Write the first draft of the application.** Use the frame on the next page to help you.

3b Now read the application again. Are you happy with it? Add or change anything that you think will improve it. **Check:** that you have not merely repeated information on the form, spelling, handwriting, use of tenses.

(4) **Work with a partner and read each other's work.**

4a What course is the writer applying for, and what experience and skills does the writer have?

4b Is there anything that you do not understand?

4c Check the application for the things in 3b. Remember it is always easier to find other people's mistakes than your own.

(5) **Lastly,** write a final draft of your application.

(6) **Follow up.**

Find out about a course you are interested in. Send off for the application form. Fill it in.

Writing Frame

Supporting statement

I am applying for the _____ course because

_____ and I would like to _____

_____

I took great pleasure in _____

_____

Since coming to this country in _____

I have _____

This _____

_____

In _____ I studied _____

and very much enjoyed _____

In my spare time I _____ This has given

me experience of _____

_____

In future I would like to _____ I feel that this

course would _____

Reports

Text 1: My favourite television programme

1 There are many nature programmes on television. I like them all but my favourite is Nature Watch.

Nature Watch is on Channel 4 on Sunday evenings, from 7.15pm to 8.15pm. It is about wild animals. Every week we see animals from different countries – tigers,
5 lizards, monkeys, wolves. The programmes can be funny and sometimes shocking.

We learn many things about the animals, for example, what they eat, how they hunt. Also, the programmes show that many animals are in danger.

Nature Watch is interesting and educational. It teaches us about the world. I watch it with my family and we all enjoy it.

Text 2: Incense

1 In India incense is everywhere. You can find it in all the houses and temples. It is an important part of Indian culture.

Incense gives off a sweet smell. It fills our homes and chases away insects, for example mosquitoes. We put incense in the temples for our Gods. In south India,
5 it is used as a medicine.

Children and old people make incense at home. They mix many kinds of wood, spices, colours and oils, and then roll the incense sticks with their hands.

Many countries produce incense but Indian incense is the best in the world.

Reading Exercises

1. **Read texts 1 and 2 and answer the following questions. Circle true or false.**

   eg Incense is used as a medicine.   true/false

   1a Nature Watch is about flowers and trees.   true/false

   1b Nature Watch is on BBC1 on Sunday evenings.   true/false

   1c Incense is a food you eat.   true/false

   1d Incense is not made by children.   true/false

2. **The writers give facts and their opinions. Find a fact and an opinion in each text.**

Text Analysis

Work with a partner.

1 **Find the introduction, the middle and the conclusion of texts 1 and 2.**

2 **Discuss the writers' purpose.**

Do you think the writers want:

2a to give only facts?

2b to give only their opinion?

2c to give facts and their opinion?

Do you think this is always true about reports?

3 **Number the paragraphs. Find which paragraph gives:**

a general statement	
Text 1:	Text 2:
facts	
Text 1:	Text 2:
examples	
Text 1:	Text 2:
how something is done	
Text 1:	Text 2:
the writer's opinion	
Text 1:	Text 2:

4 **Choose your favourite television programme and tell your partner about it, giving facts and opinions.**

Look at the differences between telling and writing about something:

How many times do you use *and* _____ ?

How many times do you use *it* _____ ?

How many examples do you give?

Language Exercises

(It) is on Channel 4.

Nature Watch

(It) teaches us about the world.

(It) fills our homes.

Incense

(It) gives off a sweet smell.

1   1a   In the Present Simple tense **he, she, it** add **-s** or **-es**.

I/you/we/they	teach
He/she/it	teaches

verbs that end in:

ch, sh, s, x, z, o

I/you/we/they	fill
He/she/it	fills

verbs that end in
other letters

1b   Read this example from text 2.

Incense fills our homes and chases insects.

2   **Find and underline the verbs in text 1 and 2.**

3   **Fill in the table, using either *-es* or *–s* and make sentences:**

Verbs	He She -s It
Work	*eg He works in London.*
Use	
Do	
Fix	
See	
Rush	
Come	
Wash	
Bring	
Watch	

Language Exercises continued

4 Change the thing or person in these sentences to *it he she* or *they.*

   eg The photos are ready.   <u>*They*</u> *are ready.*

  4a Mary is very kind.   _____ is very kind.

  4b Cars make a lot of noise.   _____ make a lot of noise.

  4c The girls like music.   _____ like music

  4d The doctor is very busy.   _____ is very busy.

  4e The war in my country is not over.   _____ is not over.

  4f Abdul wants to get a job.   _____ wants to get a job.

5 **Choose the correct form of the verb in these sentences:**

   eg The programme ~~teach~~ / teaches us about the world.

  5a The phone in the office ring/rings all day.

  5b Computers help/helps us to communicate.

  5c My son is/are at school.

  5d They come/comes back at 5 o'clock.

  5e It go/goes very fast.

6 **Look at these sentences from text 1 and 2:**

They mix many kinds of wood, spices, colours and oils.

We see wild animals from different countries: tigers, lizards, monkeys, wolves.

In English we use **commas,** when we give examples and list things.

7 **Add commas to these sentences. Use a red pen.**

   eg I eat a lot of fruit, for example, apples, bananas, grapes and oranges.

  7a In the morning she wakes up has a shower makes breakfast and takes the children to school.

  7b The days of the week are Monday Tuesday Wednesday Thursday Friday Saturday and Sunday.

  7c I like dancing singing reading and watching television.

  7d She has beautiful long black curly hair.

Writing Exercises

A good report needs:
- to be written in paragraphs
- to have an introduction, a middle and a conclusion
- to give the reader facts about a subject

it may also give the writer's opinions

The writer of a report will have a purpose: to inform the reader

① **Work with a partner. Plan a report on a television programme you both know. Work in your own language if you want.**

1a First, choose the programme and decide what facts and what opinions you want to give. Make notes:

facts   opinions

_____   _____

_____   _____

_____   _____

_____   _____

1b Next, make a plan. Decide the order for your ideas. Make notes:

title   _____

beginning   _____

             _____

middle   _____

             _____

             _____

end   _____

             _____

② **Write the report.**

2a Use the frame on the next page.

2b **Now** read your report again. Are you happy with it?

Add or change anything that will improve it. **Check:** spelling, verb endings, pronouns, commas.

2c **Lastly,** write a final draft.

③ **Follow up.** Write a report on a film or book or sport or hobby.

Writing Frame

There are many _____ _____ but _____

_____ _____ _____

_____ _____ _____

_____ is on _____ _____

It is about _____ _____ _____

_____ _____ _____

_____ _____ _____

The programme can _____ _____ _____

_____ _____ _____

_____ _____ _____

Also, _____ _____ _____ _____

_____ _____ _____

_____ _____ _____

Reports

Text 1: Observation Report Form

1   Introduction

This is a record of a visit to a Mother and Toddler Group, "Dolly Mixtures", in Barnsley, carried out in June 2000 as part of the Diploma in Playgroup Practice Course.

2   Description

2a   Organisation

There are 15 children, aged 16 months to 2 $\frac{1}{2}$ years of age, on the register. The session runs from 9.30 – 11.30 am on Tuesdays, Wednesdays and Fridays. The parents or carers are present while the children attend. Some younger siblings, mainly babies, also come. Parents run the group for themselves without a formal organiser but there are three mothers who take responsibility for running the group. The sessions are held in a bright, well-heated, local Scout hut.

2b   The session

When the parents enter, they write their names in the register and pay 50p for the session. They also enter what they and their children wish to drink in a different book. There is free play from 9.30 – 11.00 am. Toys are arranged into play areas, for example dressing-up clothes in one corner, books in another etc … After this, the toys are cleared away in preparation for a singing session. The chairs are arranged in a circle and songs are then sung for half an hour, led by one of the parents who helps to run the group.

3   Evaluation

3.1 Strengths

- The toys appeared to be in good condition and there were many 'push and pull' toys, as well as, puzzles, books, paints etc…The room was large enough to allow children to run around freely and choose different play areas.

- No parent or child is refused entry to the group and there are toys and books that show a range of cultures and races.

3.2 Areas for development

- More parents could be encouraged to help run the sessions, for instance to set up the room or prepare drinks.

- Children could be taught songs in other languages by parents who speak those languages.

4   Conclusion

This is a self-help, non-profit making group. It gives parents and carers the opportunity to socialise while their children play. It meets local needs, particularly those of isolated young mothers. It also provides a good stepping-stone towards more structured, pre-school education for the rising 3 year olds.

Text 2: Work Experience Report

1 Placement

I spent two weeks, from 1/11/00 to 12/11/00, doing work experience at the Film Place, Barnet.

Description of Employer

5 The Film Place is an old, independent cinema in north London. The premises are small and consist of a booking hall, an auditorium, a projection room and bar/cafe. There are five permanent members of staff but only two are full-time: the manager and projectionist. The cinema was built in 1926 and is one of the oldest in Britain.

Description of Placement

10 During the two weeks at the Film Place I worked in different parts of the organisation, shadowing and doing various jobs. I began work everyday at 12.30pm and finished between 8.30 and 10.30pm, depending on my duties. I assisted in selling tickets, answering telephone enquiries and checking tickets at the door. I also showed people to their seats and worked in the cafe/bar.

15 In the second week I worked with the projectionist who showed me how to check the equipment – projector, spools, reels. He also taught me how to prepare films ready for projection and I assisted him in the showing of a number of films, working the projector myself.

Evaluation

20 I have learnt a great deal from the work experience, in particular the importance of teamwork.
The cinema staff were very helpful and patient and I enjoyed working with them. The general duties, such as showing people to their seats, were not difficult and became routine. I particularly liked working in the projection room. This was a more
25 challenging task than some of the others as I needed to concentrate and be very precise.

I now realise how tiring a job can be but I also know that it can be very enjoyable, especially when you work with people you get on well with and that you like.

Reading Exercises

1   Read the title and headings of each report. Discuss the meaning of the titles and headings.

2   Read both texts and answer the following questions:

Text 1   **2a**   What is a Mother and Toddler group?
           2b   Is the group well-organised?

Text 2   **2c**   What is the working environment of The Film Place like?
           2d   Was it a positive or a negative experience ?

Text Analysis

1   What do you think is the purpose of a report? Is it:

1a to give personal opinions about something?

1b to describe an event?

1c to give facts about an event or a subject?

1d to criticise a person or event?

1e to analyse an event or a subject, giving facts, opinions and reasons?

2   Work with a partner. Look at texts 1 and 2 and answer the following questions. Write short notes.

2a List the main and sub-headings in each text.

2b How does the information in each paragraph link with the headings?

2c What is the purpose of the headings in the reports?

2d What are the main tenses used in the different sections of each report?

2e Why is the Simple Past used as well as the Simple Present?

3   Would it be relevant to add the following facts and opinions to text 2:

3a What the writer had for lunch each day?   Yes / no

3b What the projectionist looked like?   Yes / no

3c What the writer did not like about the placement?   Yes / no

If you answered **yes** to the last statement, under which heading would you put it and after which paragraph?

4   4a Look at the paragraph structure in text 1:

"The toys appeared to be in good condition and there were many 'push and pull' toys, as well as, puzzles, books, paints etc…"

The writer makes a statement + gives more specific information + gives examples

4b Can you find a similar structure in other paragraphs in texts 1 and 2?

4c Re-arrange these sentences into a logical paragraph:

• The classes are held in the local College.

• I go to English classes in Bradford.

• It is quite near the bus station.

• There are students from all over the world, Pakistan, Somalia, Colombia, Kosovo etc…

5   5a Make a spoken report to your partner about the English classes you attend.

5b What are the differences between a spoken and a written report?

• is the language more or less formal in a written report? Give some examples.

• do you structure the information in the same way?

• how often do you use 'and' and 'it' in a spoken report?

Language Exercises

Look at these examples from texts 1 and 2

The cinema **was built** in 1926

Sessions **are held** in a Scout hut

Both verbs are in the passive

1   1a Compare these 2 sentences:

   Somebody built the cinema in 1926   (Active)
   subject   *object*

   The cinema was built in 1926   (Passive)
   subject

   In the passive sentence we focus on **what happened.**
   In the active sentence we focus on **who did it.**

   1b In written reports the passive is commonly used as **what happened is more important than who did something.** It is also considered more concise and formal

2   2a To form the passive:

   to be   +   past participle of
                    main verb

   It is   made

   It was   made

Present Simple Passive	Past Simple Passive
I am loved	I was loved
you are loved	you were loved
he/she/it is loved	he/she/it was loved
we are loved	we were loved
you (pl) are loved	you (pl) were loved
they are loved	they were loved

Language Exercises continued

2b To change the tense in the passive, you must change the tense of 'to be', the helping or auxiliary verb. The past participle of the main verb stays the same. Remember that regular verbs add -ed to form the past participle eg *I am loved*. However, irregular verbs have irregular past participles: eg *The cake was eaten.*

2c Find all the examples of the passive in texts 1 and 2 and underline them.

2d Fill in this table, giving the Present and Past Simple Passive of the verbs:

Verb	Present Simple Passive	Past Simple Passive
eg make	it *is made*	it *was made*
eg build	they *are built*	they
say	it	it
report	it	it
damage	they	they
take	it	it

3

3a Complete the sentences, using one of these verbs in the Present Simple Passive:

show   cancel   make   cause   clean   employ

eg   Yogurt is made from milk.

i   A cinema is a place where films _____.

ii   Many deaths _____ by dangerous driving.

iii It is a small shop, only 3 people _____ there.

iv   In this hotel, the rooms _____ every week.

v   All the trains _____ because of the fog.

3b Re-write these sentences using the Past Simple Passive.
All the sentences are in the active.

eg People advised us not to go there.

We were advised not to go there.

i   Builders built this house in 1990.

ii   A person posted the letter last week.

iii A person shot a policeman outside a Post Office.

iv   The South African people elected President Mandela.

v   A thief stole my bag last night.

Writing Exercises

A good report needs:

- to be written in paragraphs
- to have an introduction, a middle and a conclusion, using headings when appropriate
- to analyse an event or subject, giving facts, opinions and reasons.

The writer of a report will have a purpose: to analyse a subject and inform the reader.

① **Work with a partner. Plan a report on the College or Institute where you attend classes. Work in your own language to plan if you prefer.**

1a First, decide what facts and what opinions you want to give. Make a list.

facts   opinions

_____   _____

_____   _____

_____   _____

1b Next, make a written plan and decide the order for your ideas:

title   _____

beginning _____

           _____

middle   _____

           _____

           _____

end   _____

           _____

1c Decide on the use of headings. Will you use them? What will they focus on?

② **2a Write the first draft of your report.** Use the frame on the next page to help you.

2b Now read your report again. Are you happy with it? Add or change anything that will improve it. **Check:** spelling, passives, sequencing words and phrases.

③ **Work with a partner and read each other's work.**

3a What is the writer reporting about and why?

3b Is there anything that you do not understand?

3c Check it for the things in 2b. Remember it is always easier to find other people's mistakes than your own.

④ **Lastly,** write a final draft.

⑤ **Follow up.** Write a report on services in your local area.

Writing Frame

_____

Introduction

This is a report on _____

where I _____

Description

_____ is _____

There are _____

It is _____

My classes _____

I _____

After this I _____

and then I _____

Evaluation

I have _____

_____ I _____

like _____ but _____

_____

_____

Discussion Essays

Text 1: TV is Bad for Children

1 Some people think tv is bad for children. Other people do not agree.

I believe some tv programmes are good. They can teach children many things. A good example is nature films. Also tv can help many children learn English. Some children's programmes are fun.

5 Other people do not agree. They think many programmes are violent and use bad language. They believe children stop reading because they prefer watching tv.

On balance, I think that there are many good programmes for children but sometimes they watch too much tv every day. In my opinion, parents must control the television in their home.

Text 2: Down with Cars

1 Cars are dirty and noisy. Cars kill people. Some people ask, why do we have them?

A lot of people hate cars. They believe cars are bad for society. Cars pollute the air and the pollution from cars causes many illnesses, for example asthma. Many 5 people die each year in car accidents. Some people think we need more buses and trains. They say we do not need cars.

On the other hand, cars are fast and save time. People have jobs in factories making cars. Cars are cheaper than trains.

In conclusion, I believe cars are bad for society but I think we need them. In the future we need cars that are cleaner and safer than cars today.

Reading Exercises

Text 1

   1a Read the title and the first sentence of each paragraph. What do you think the writer will say?

   1b Now read all the text. Does the writer think tv is bad for children?

   1c What is your opinion? Give reasons.

Text 2

   1d Read the text.

   1e Make a list of opinions for and against cars.

   1f What is the writer's opinion? Do you agree? Give reasons.

Text Analysis

Work with a partner:

1   1a   **Look at texts 1 and 2 and find the introduction, the middle and the conclusion.**

    1b   **Answer these questions and discuss your answers.**

Write the first sentence. Does this link to the title? Is this important in the introduction?   Text 1:
Text 2:
How many opinions are there, for and against? What are the opinions?   Text 1:
Text 2:
Write the last sentence. Is it a good last sentence?   Text 1:
Text 2:
Is the writer for or against?   Text 1:
Text 2:
What is the main tense? Give an example. Why does the writer use *this* tense?   Text 1:
Text 2:

2   **Look at the difference between telling someone your opinion and writing about it. Would you say or write these phrases? Tick the right box.**

	speaking	writing	both
a What a load of rubbish	☐	☐	☐
b Some people think	☐	☐	☐
c In my opinion	☐	☐	☐
d I don't think	☐	☐	☐

Language Exercises

1 Useful language for discussions:

the writer's opinions	I believe I think I feel In my opinion In my view Also			
other people's opinions	a lot of some many other	people		think believe feel agree
	a lot of some many other	people	do not	think believe feel agree
conclusions	On balance In conclusion			

1a Find these in the texts and underline them.

1b Fill the gaps using words and phrases from the boxes. You can use more than one word in each gap.

Some people think tv is bad for children. _____ do not agree.

_____ some tv programmes are good. They can teach children many things.

_____ . They think many programmes are violent and use bad language.

_____ , I think that there are many good programmes for children but sometimes they watch too much tv every day. _____, parents must control the television in their home.

Language Exercises continued

2   Put these words in the right order to make sentences.

eg *Africa In than my safer opinion is Britain*
     In my opinion Africa is safer than Britain.

2a television I much feel too children watch

2b me A with lot agree of not people do

2c work Some not people should think mothers

2d society cars In for conclusion bad I are believe

3   Read these opinions.

I think chocolate is bad for you. / I do not think chocolate is bad for you.

She believes meat is good for you. / She does not believe meat is good for you.

Give the opposite opinion:

eg *I hate cars / I do not hate cars.*

3a She believes in God / _____

3b We do not feel happy today / _____

3c I think she loves him / _____

3d He does not agree with her / _____

4   In discussions it is useful to compare facts and ideas, eg cars are cheaper than trains.

4a Look at these sentences and work out the patterns for comparing in English. Discuss your ideas with a partner.

   i   Cars are faster than buses.
        Buses are cheaper than trains.

   ii   Trains are more expensive than buses.
        London is more polluted than Cambridge.

4b Make sentences comparing these things:

   bikes (slow) cars

   air travel (expensive) road travel

   motorbikes (dangerous) cars

   walking (healthier) driving

Writing Exercises

A good discussion essay needs:
- to be written in paragraphs
- to have an introduction, a middle and a conclusion
- to give your opinion and other people's opinions.

① **Work with a partner or alone.** Plan a discussion essay.

1a First, choose one of these titles:

Children today have too much money

People should not eat meat

'An eye for an eye' is the best punishment

1b Next, think of

your opinions	other people's opinions

1c Then, decide on the order for your ideas. Make short notes:

title _____

introduction _____

_____

your ideas _____

_____

other people's ideas _____

_____

conclusion _____

_____

② **2a Write the essay.** Use the frame on the next page to help you.

2b Now, read your essay again. Are you happy with it? Add or change anything that will improve it. **Check:** spelling, word order, comparisons, capital letters and full stops.

2c Write a final draft.

③ **Follow up.** Write about something you feel strongly about.

Writing Frame

_____

Some people think _____

_____ Other people _____

_____

In my opinion _____

_____

Also, _____

_____

I think _____

_____

Other people feel _____

They believe _____

On balance, I think _____

_____

_____

Discussion Essays

Text 1: 'Man is Destroying his Environment' Discuss

1 Is man destroying his environment? Many people are worried about the quality of the air, the water and the land around us. Are we doing enough to protect our planet? Is it too late to save it?

The growth of industry throughout the 20th century has caused a great deal of pollution
5 which is harming the world-wide environment. Research shows that the three main effects of pollution are: damage to the ozone layer, global warming and acid rain. Smoke from factories and car exhaust fumes have led to holes in the ozone layer and an increase in the world's temperature. Acid rain drops dangerous chemicals on the land and seas. Also, the industrial waste and the use of aerosol sprays, containing
10 CFCs, harms the environment. The majority of conservationists believe that governments are not doing enough to protect the earth from the harmful effects of man-made pollution. They state that profit and the desire for high standards of living are the main concern of politicians.

On the other hand, some people would argue that efforts to control pollution are
15 beginning to show results. There are now stricter laws to limit waste and save resources, for example the use of lead-free petrol and the ban on burning coal and wood in cities. People are more aware of pollution as a problem, children are taught about it in school. It is claimed there are many local schemes for recycling waste and for protecting wildlife. These are helping to protect the environment from further damage.
20 However, 'green' organisations state that it is too little, too late. They point to the changes in weather throughout the world, as well as the growth in industrial pollution in many developing countries. Conservationists believe that radical political solutions are needed.

On balance, I would agree that pollution continues to threaten the planet, although in
25 my opinion many governments are now taking the matter more seriously. Furthermore, there is greater awareness and more controls than fifty years ago. Nevertheless, we need governments to act now to save the planet in the 21st century. Pollution is created by people, people must do something to stop it.

Text 2: A Woman's Place?

1 Some people believe that a woman's place is in the home. In fact it is such a widely held view that it has become an idiom in the English language. For many years nobody questioned this opinion and social conventions supported the view. In the 1970s, the Women's Liberation Movement and feminist writers began to challenge this attitude
5 and the role of women in Britain began to change. As a South American man, I question these changes.

As I see it, the wife is the queen of the home while the man is the most important person in the family. When he gets married, a man promises to look after his wife and children, in sickness and in health, in the good times and the bad times. Therefore, he goes out
10 to work to bring home wages for food and clothes. His wife's job is to stay at home and look after the house and the children, cooking and cleaning. She should also help the children with their homework. For all this hard work she deserves respect and the care and devotion of her husband. If she did not do this, who would take care of the home?

Others would argue that jobs outside the home for both is a good thing because it gives
15 the husband and the wife a sense of independence. It is also claimed that women's financial contribution when they bring home wages is very important for the security of the family. However, I think jobs for both is a mistake. When the wife begins to work it is the beginning of a broken marriage. In the first place, when the wife works she looks for new friends, fashionable clothes and more fun. As a result she starts to forget
20 the children's care, the husband and the home. For South American people I am in favour of the husband at work and the wife at home. They are used to this way of living.

In conclusion, a woman's place is in the home. Money is not a good reason to change the way men and women have behaved for many centuries. Money only calms the nerves.

Reading Exercises

1 **Read the titles of each text.** What do you think the writers might say? Now read the texts and see if you predicted correctly.

2 **Underline words or phrases you do not know and discuss them** with your teacher or look them up in a dictionary.

3 **Text 1 - Does the writer agree or disagree with the title?** Make a list of the advantages and disadvantages mentioned in the text. Which is the strongest argument?

4 **Text 2 - What is the writer's opinion?** Do you agree? Discuss with a partner.

Text Analysis

1   1a Examine these headings.

- stating the problem/introducing the subject
- giving personal opinion and reasons for that opinion
- giving other people's views and disagreeing with them
- summarising and concluding

1b Match the paragraphs in text 1 and 2 to a heading.

2   Go back to Text 1 and Text 2 and underline the first sentence of each paragraph. These are often called 'the topic sentence'. What is the role of the topic sentence? What is the link between the topic sentences and the headings in exercise 1a?

3   Look at Text 1 What arguments does the writer use? Use the mind map to make notes.

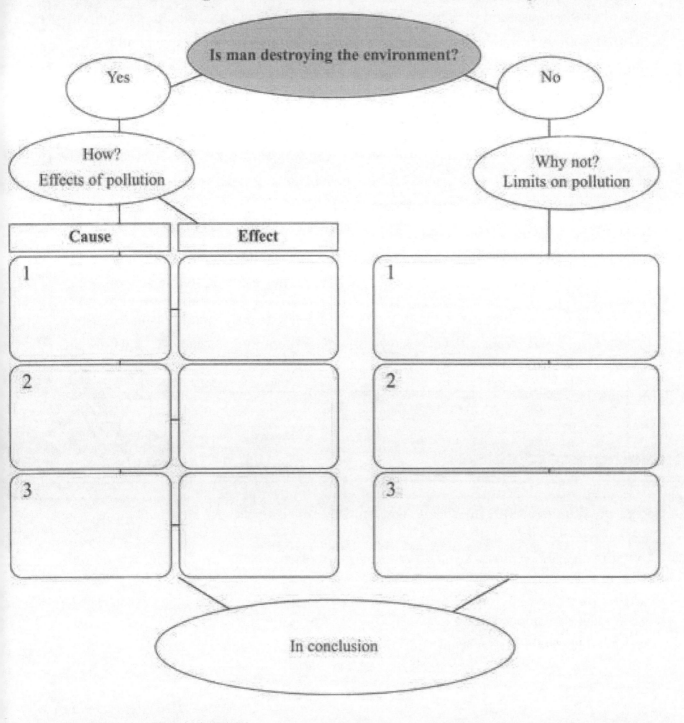

Text Analysis continued

4   Look at paragraph 2 of Text 2.

The topic sentence is a general statement.	*As I see it, the wife is the queen of the home while the man is the most important person in the family.*
Notice how the next 2 sentences develop the topic and give examples.	*When he gets married, a man promises to look after his wife and children, in sickness and in health, in the good times and the bad times. Therefore, he goes out to work to bring home wages for food and clothes.*

This is a common way to structure a paragraph

   i)   general statement

   ii) development of the statement and specific examples.

Find a paragraph in Text 1 that follows this pattern.

5   **With a partner, discuss what you think about the role of men and women in the home. Which is more formal, writing or speaking?**

Would you say or write these phrases? Tick the right box.

		speaking	writing	both
5a	That's a load of sexist clap trap.	☐	☐	☐
5b	Others would argue that ...	☐	☐	☐
5c	I think ...	☐	☐	☐
5d	Do you really think so?	☐	☐	☐
5e	Research shows that ...	☐	☐	☐
5f	I see what you're saying, but ...	☐	☐	☐

Language Exercises

1 **1a In discussion essays in English these are common ways of introducing a subject:**

    i)   Should children watch less tv?
            problem expressed as a question

    ii)   Some people believe that children should watch less tv.
            general statement

    iii)   It is important to consider the advantages and disadvantages
            of television for children.
            readers asked to consider both sides

1b In your language would you introduce a subject in the same way? If not, what would you say?

1c Write the first sentence for the following essays three times using the examples in a, b and c.

    • Children today have too much money

    • People should not eat meat

    • An eye for an eye is the best punishment

2 **The following are useful phrases and expressions for discussion essays:**

Stating personal opinions	I think / believe/feel that In my opinion / view I am convinced that It seems to me that I think that To my mind As I see it As far as I am concerned I am in favour of / I am against/ I am opposed to
Giving reasons and ordering the reasons	There are a number of reasons why In the first place / Firstly Also It should also be noted that Lastly
Giving other people's view and disagreeing with it	On the other hand, some people feel / believe /think Others would argue that Another claim often made is that However, nevertheless / although
Summarising and concluding	On balance / One could say that To sum up It is my belief that To conclude / In conclusion

2a Find and highlight these phrases in texts 1 and 2.

Language Exercises continued

3 **Put the words in the correct order to make meaningful sentences.**

   3a children in too television opinion watch my much

   3b there it is pollution seems me a of lot that to Britain in

   3c believe capital I punishment that thing is good a

   3d mistake I a think is jobs both for

4 **Fill in the gaps with the correct words and phrases:**

Is man destroying his environment? [1]_____ are worried about the quality of the air, the water and the land around us. Are we doing enough to protect our planet? Is it too late to save it?

The growth of industry throughout the 20th century has [2]_____ a great deal of pollution which is harming the world-wide environment. [3]_____ that the three main effects of pollution are: damage to the ozone layer, global warming and acid rain. Smoke from factories and car exhaust fumes have [4]_____ holes in the ozone layer and an increase in the world's temperature. Acid rain drops dangerous chemicals on the land and seas. [5]_____, the industrial waste and the use of aerosol sprays, containing CFCs, harms the environment. The majority of conservationists [6]_____ that governments are not doing enough to protect the earth from the harmful [7]_____ of man-made pollution. They [8]_____ that profit and the desire for high standards of living are the main concern of politicians.

[9]_____, some people would [10]_____ that efforts to control pollution are beginning to show results. There are now stricter laws to limit waste and save resources ____ [11]_____ the use of lead-free petrol and the ban on burning coal and wood in cities. People are more aware of pollution as a problem, children are taught about it in school. They [12]_____ that there are many local schemes for recycling waste and for protecting wildlife. These are helping to protect the environment from further damage. [13]_____, 'green' organisations state that it is too little, too late. They [14]_____ the changes in weather throughout the world, [15]_____ the growth in industrial pollution in many developing countries. Conservationists [16]_____ that radical political solutions are needed.

[17]_____, I would [18]_____ that pollution continues to threaten the planet, although in my opinion many governments are now taking the matter more seriously. [19]_____, there is greater awareness and more controls than fifty years ago. [20]_____, we need governments to act now to save the planet in the 21st century. Pollution is created by people, people must do something to stop it.

Writing Exercises

A good discussion essay needs:

- to have an introduction, a middle and a conclusion
- to be written in paragraphs
- to keep to the point
- to give the writer's opinion and other people's views
- to come to conclusions

① Work with a partner or alone. Plan a discussion essay. Use your own language to plan if you want.

1a First, choose one of these titles
Children today have too much money
People should not eat meat
'An eye for an eye' is the best punishment

1b Next, think of all the arguments for and against.

1c Then, decide on the order for your ideas:

title

introduction

your ideas

other people's ideas

conclusion

② 2a Write the essay. Use the frame on the next page to help you.

2b Work with a partner. Read your essays together and discuss if there is anything you want to add or change.   Check: order of ideas
clarity
variety of expressions
grammar   tense, conditionals
spelling
punctuation

③ Write a final draft.

④ Follow up

Write about something you feel strongly about

Writing Frame

_____

Some people think that _____

_____

_____

In my opinion _____

_____

_____

_____

_____

As I see it _____

_____

There are a number of reasons why _____

_____ In the first place _____

_____ Also, _____

On the other hand, some people feel that _____

Another claim made is that _____

_____

However, _____

_____

_____

In conclusion, _____

_____

_____

Comparative Essay

Text 1: Family Life in Morocco

1 A Moroccan family is very different from a European family. In Morocco the family is bigger and stays together.

For example, in Morocco it is very rare to find old people living alone. They usually stay with their children or grandchildren or other members of the family.
5 However, in Europe old people often live alone, or in homes.

In Morocco, when a girl gets married she goes to live with her husband's family. However in Europe, the girl and her husband usually live together, just the two of them.

These are just a few things one can say about a Moroccan family.

Text 2: Comparing Bangladesh and England

1 I come from Bangladesh. It is in the south east of Asia. Bangladesh is very different to England.

Bangladesh is much hotter than England and much wetter. We often have terrible floods, thousands of people die. Because there is a lot of water, people travel by
5 boat. The rivers are our motorways.

Bangladesh is more fertile than England, and we grow rice and other crops. Food is much cheaper than in England, and I think it tastes better too.

Bangladesh is a very beautiful country, and I am happy that I grew up there.

Reading Exercises

1 1a Read the titles of Texts 1 and 2. What do you think the writers will say?

   1b Now read the texts. Were you right?

   1c Read Text 1. Find two differences between families in Morocco and England.

   1d Read Text 2. Find two differences between Bangladesh and England.

2 Highlight any words you still do not understand, and ask another student or your teacher.

Text Analysis

1   Work with a partner.

1a Look at texts 1 and two and find the introduction, the middle and the conclusion.

1b Answer these questions and discuss your answers:

Write the first sentence. Does this link to the title? Is this important in an introduction?
Text 1:
Text 2:
How many things does the writer compare?
Text 1:
Text 2:
Write the last sentence. Is it a good last sentence?
Text 1:
Text 2:
What is the main tense? Give an example. Why does the writer use this tense?
Text 1:
Text 2:

2   Match these headings with each paragraph.

Text 1   conclusion   old people   introduction   married couples

Text 2   weather   transport   introduction   conclusion   food

3   Work with a partner.

Tell your partner about a country you know well and compare it with England. Look at the difference between comparing *when you speak* and *when you write.*

How many times do you use *and* _____ ?

How many times do you use *it* _____ ?

Which is more formal, writing or speaking?

Language Exercises

1 **1a Look at this sentence.**

Bangladesh is *hotter than* England.

Work with a partner. Make sentences comparing Bangladesh and England. Say the sentences aloud first, then write them down.
Use these words   hot, cold, wet, dry, poor, rich, cheap.

1b Look at this sentence.

Bangladesh is *more fertile* than England.

Work with a partner. Make sentences comparing Bangladesh and England. Say the sentences aloud first, then write them down.
Use these words   beautiful, expensive, crowded.

1c When do you use *...er* as in *cheaper* and when do you use *more* as in *more expensive*?

1d Make five sentences comparing England and one other country. Say the sentences aloud first, then write them down.

_____   _____   _____

_____   _____   _____

_____   _____   _____

_____   _____   _____

_____   _____   _____

_____   _____   _____

_____   _____   _____

_____

2 **Fill the gaps using the words in the box.**

eg *Food tastes better in Bangladesh*

2a Food costs _____ in England than in Bangladesh.

2b Floods are _____ in Bangladesh.

2c In Bangladesh, the roads are used _____ than the rivers.

2d Bangladeshi food tastes _____ than English food.

> more   less   better   worse

Language Exercises continued

3   Join these sentences using *but*. Remember to change full stops and capital letters.

   eg   It is hot in Bangladesh   The weather in England is cold

   *It is hot in Bangladesh **but** the weather in England is cold*

   3a   In Morocco old people live   In England old people live alone
            with their children

   _____

   3b   English people travel on the roads   In Bangladesh they use the rivers

   _____

   3c   Moroccan families live together   In England families live apart

   _____

   3d   England has a water shortage   There are floods in Bangladesh

   _____

   3e   Farmers grow rice in Bangladesh   English farmers grow corn and wheat

   _____

4   Now write the sentences again, using *however*. Look at what happens to the full stops and capital letters.

   eg   It is hot in Bangladesh   The weather in England is cold.

      *It is hot in Bangladesh. **However**, the weather in England is cold*

Writing Exercises

A good comparative essay needs:
- to be written in paragraphs
- to have an introduction, a middle and a conclusion
- to compare different points

① **Work with a partner or alone. Plan a comparative essay.**

1a First, choose one of these titles:
Food in England and another country
Family life in England and another country
A general comparison between England and another country

1b Next, break down the subject into different points. Make notes about each point in each country.

Point 1 (eg weather)
England
Other country
Point 2
England
Other country
Point 3
England
Other country

1c Then, decide what you will put in the introduction and conclusion. Make short notes.

② **2a Write the essay.** Use the frame on the next page.

2b Now, read your essay again. Are you happy with it? Add or change anything that will improve it. **Check:** spelling, comparisons, word order, capital letters and full stops.

2c Write a final draft.

③ **Follow up.**

Work on your own this time, and write another of the essays listed in 1a.

Writing Frame

_____

_____ is different from _____

_____

_____

In England_____

_____

However, in _____

_____

English _____

_____but _____

_____

In _____

_____

However _____

_____

I think that _____ is better because _____

_____

_____

Comparative Essay

Text 1: A Comparison of the Education Systems in England and India

1 Although India is one of the largest democracies in the world the right to free education is still not available to all. In sharp contrast, education in England is not only free but compulsory between the ages of 5 and 16.

The age groups in nursery, primary and secondary schools are very similar in the Indian
5 and English systems. Children start school at about 4 years old and finish secondary at either 16 or 18 years of age. The main difference is that in the English system until children are 16 they automatically move up to the next class at the end of the year, whereas in the Indian system the students who fail the end of year exams are made to repeat the year. The embarrassment of failing encourages the students to work harder.

10 The subjects (Maths, Science, English, History, Geography, Art, PE, Music, Design Technology etc) up to 16 years are again quite similar in both the systems. However, the English put more emphasis on IT and in India children have to learn both a regional language and English.

The methods of teaching in both countries are quite different. In India, the students sit in
15 rows and face the teacher. They mainly copy from the blackboard, learn by rote and use textbooks. In England the teaching methods are more student-centred, with group activities and project work. This encourages children to find out things for themselves. These methods help in the overall development of a child's personality. The disadvantage is that the atmosphere in the class is informal which can lead to discipline problems.

20 Assessment methods are also different. In India, the method of assessing what students have learnt is through examinations. These are taken at least every year. Whereas in England students are continuously observed and assessed. They also sit exams. This system seems more complicated and the teachers spend a lot of time on keeping records and filling in paper work.

25 It would seem that there are good and bad things about both systems. However, both in India and in England the systems are changing to cope with changes in society.

Text 2: The country or the city - which is better?

1 In our street in London there are very few families with children. There are old people and there are young couples who have not yet had children or who have babies. But as soon as the babies start to walk, their parents move them to a better life in the countryside. But does the countryside really give them a better life? In this essay I will
5 compare the benefits of country and city living.

For families with children the countryside is considered better because there is more space. Housing is often cheaper than in the city, and gardens are bigger, so children have more room to run around. There are woods and fields where children can explore, build 'dens' and play independently of their parents. In the city children are more
10 controlled, they have to go to playgrounds, be in their gardens or else play in the streets. This means they cannot develop independence as early as in the country.

It is argued that the countryside has a better environment for living than the city. You can find beautiful views, and wide open spaces. There is peace and quiet and clean air. In contrast the city produces noise from traffic and people, pollution, and a feeling of
15 being shut in.

However, facilities are certainly much better in cities than in the countryside. There is always a hospital, doctor's surgery or dentist within easy travelling distance. There is a choice of schools, colleges and universities. And for entertainment there are theatres, cinemas, concert halls, clubs, leisure centres and sports fields. Whereas in the country
20 people may have to travel long distances to find any one of these. And all of these facilities create jobs.

To sum up, it seems that the countryside provides a good environment for children as they grow up but when they become young adults then the city, with its facilities and jobs, is a better place to live.

Reading exercises

1 Read the titles of both texts. With a partner, make notes of the things you think the writer will compare.

2 Now read the first and last sentence of each paragraph. Make any changes to your notes.

3 Finally, read both texts. What things did each writer compare? Were your first thoughts correct?

4 Write down all the words you do not understand, and ask another student to explain them, look them up in your dictionary, or ask the teacher.

Text Analysis

Work with a partner.

1 **1a Examine these headings for Text 1:**
- teaching methods
- summarising and concluding
- age groups
- introducing the subject
- assessment
- subjects

1b Match the paragraphs in text 1 to a heading.

1c Which tense do both writers use? Why do they use this tense? Can you think of an example where you would use a different tense for a comparative essay?

2 **2a Match the phrases in the box with the sentences from paragraph 5, Text 1.**

example from India / opinion / general statement /example from England	
	Assessment methods are also different.
	In India, the method of assessing what students have learnt is through examinations. These are taken at least every year.
	Whereas in England students are continuously observed and assessed. They also sit exams.
	This system seems more complicated and the teachers spend a lot of time on keeping records and filling in paper work.

2b Find another paragraph from Text 1 that follows the same order.

3 **3a Tell your partner about where you live now, comparing it with somewhere else you know well.**

3b Think about the differences between a spoken and written comparison:

- do you use full sentences when you speak?
- how often do you use 'and' or 'it' when speaking?
- do you use phrases such as 'however' or 'whereas' when you speak?
- what do you use instead of 'however'?

3c Look at the texts again. Can you find other words or phrases that you use more often in writing than in speaking?

Language Exercises

1 **1a Look at this sentence from Text 2:**

In this essay I will compare the benefits of country and city living.
Do you use a similar sentence when you write an essay in your language?

2 **Look at the table of useful phrases in the exercises on discussion essays (page 116) for help with expressions for stating opinions, giving reasons, summarising and concluding.**

3 **Fill the gaps.**

eg The countryside is a *better* environment *than* the city.

3a Housing is _____ in the country _____ in the city.

3b Gardens in the country are _____ _____ in the city.

3c Pollution is _____ in the city _____ in the country.

3d Communities are _____ in the country _____ in the city.

3e In the city children's play is _____ controlled _____ in the country.
Make three more sentences comparing the city and the countryside, giving your own opinion.

4 **Writers often use these expressions when they compare things:**

are/is the same as, are/is similar to , are/is different to/from,

4a Find examples of these expressions in the texts and highlight them.

4b Use one of these expressions to join these sentences comparing Indian and English education:

eg The age for starting school in England *is the same* as the age for starting school in India.

The subject range in India _____ that in England.

The languages learnt in England _____ the languages learnt in India.

The teaching methods used in India _____ the methods in England.

The leaving age in India is _____ the age that English children leave school.

4c Finish these sentences.

When comparing the Indian and English education systems, similarities include

_____

When comparing the Indian and English education systems, differences include

_____

Now write two sentences giving differences and similarities between the education system in England now and the one you experienced as a child.

Language Exercises continued

5 **Writers often use these expressions when they contrast things:**

however, in contrast, whereas, but, on the one hand....on the other hand

5a Find examples of these expressions in the texts and highlight them.

5b Use one of these expressions to join these sentences and make a contrast. Remember to change full stops and capital letters where necessary.

Chinese food is tasty.	English food is dull.
Cities usually have lots of buses.	Public transport is poor in the country.
In Indian schools children respect the teacher.	In English schools discipline is poor.
Housing is a big problem in London.	In the north of England there are plenty of cheap houses and flats to rent.

6 **When you are writing an essay you do not just give your own opinion, you often say what other people are thinking too.**

6a What is the difference between these two ways of saying what people think?

People consider that the countryside is better for families with children.
For families with children, the countryside is considered better.

The writer has used one of these. Why do you think she has used this one? Find it in the text.

6b Change these expressions from the passive to the active. See pages 102 and 103.

eg Facilities are considered to be better.
      People consider facilities to be better.

A sense of community is thought to be stronger in the country.

_____

Cities are thought to be lonely places.

_____

Tales are told of old people who die alone.

_____

It is argued the countryside is cleaner.

_____

6c Change these expressions from the active to the passive.

eg People say that housing is cheap in the country.
      It is said that housing is cheap in the country.

People argue that children have more freedom in the country.

People consider transport is better in the city.

Some people think that cities are lonely places.

People say the country is safer than the city.

Writing Exercises

A good comparative essay needs:

• to have an introduction, a middle and a conclusion

• to be written in paragraphs

• to analyse and compare different points

• to keep to the point

• to come to conclusions

(1) **Work with a partner or alone. Plan a comparative essay.**

1a Choose one of the following:
Education in England now and your education as a child
Food in England and one other country
Family life in England and one other country

1b Now, think of all the different areas of the subject that you will compare. Use mind map (a) to help you plan. Mind map (b) is an example.

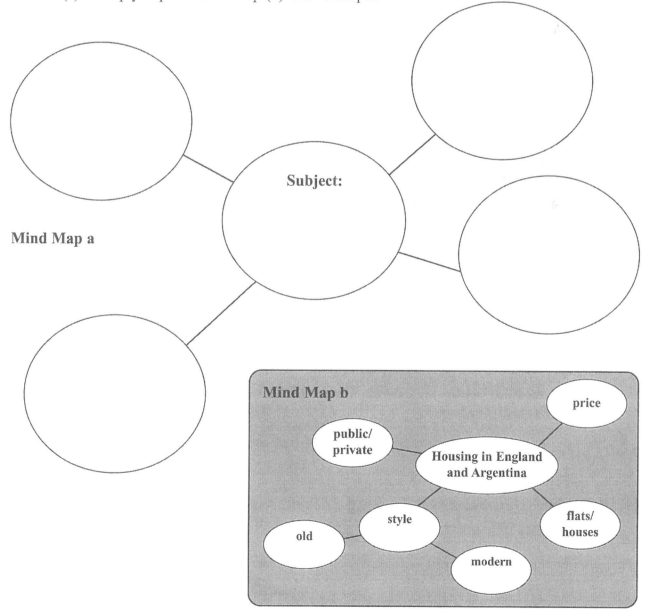

Mind Map a

Subject:

Mind Map b

price

public/private

Housing in England and Argentina

style

old

modern

flats/houses

Writing Exercises continued

1c Then, decide on the order for your ideas.

title	
introduction	
first area for comparison	
next area for comparison	
third area for comparison	
Conclusion	

(2) **Write the first draft of the essay.**

2a Use the frame on the next page to help you.

2b Now read the essay again. Are you happy with it? Add or change anything that you think will improve it. **Check:** order of ideas
  clarity
  variety of expressions
  grammar – tense, comparatives, passives
  spelling
  punctuation

(3) **Work with a partner and read each other's work.**

3a What is the writer comparing, and what different areas does the writer compare?

3b Is there anything that you do not understand?

3c Check the essay for the things in 2b. Remember it is always easier to find other people's mistakes than your own.

(4) **Lastly,** write a final draft of your essay.

(5) **Follow up**

Write an essay of your choice, comparing two things.

Writing Frame

In England there are _____

_____

In this essay, I will compare _____

_____

The _____ in England _____

_____

In contrast _____

_____

The _____ in _____

_____

Whereas _____

_____

Finally _____

_____

In conclusion _____

_____

Appendix
A genre approach to teaching writing for ESOL Students

What is a genre approach to writing ?

For the last ten years there has been considerable, often heated debate amongst linguists and educationalists on the application of genre theory to the classroom, in particular the primary school classroom. Passionate advocacy has met with robust criticism, yet at its heart lies a deeper issue of equity and the role of education to empower.

Genre theory states that pieces of writing which share a common purpose will tend to share a common structure and common language patterns. A genre approach to teaching writing can be defined as a way of analysing the generic textual and linguistic features of writing produced for similar purposes and similar contexts and then supporting students to reproduce these features.

Genre theory has its origins in the linguistic theories of M A K Halliday and its pedagogical applications in Australia, and more recently in Britain, the USA and other countries. Hallidayan linguistics are complex but an understanding of his general principles are interesting and important when considering the background to genre. Halliday argues that linguistics should not abstract itself from the study of meaning. He sees language as a social phenomenon with a purpose or function behind all communication. He maintains that communication takes place because of what people already know, and when speakers engage in interactions they make predictions, using situational and linguistic clues available to them in the given situation. Language use is thus intimately linked to context and it is his view that participants make choices about language, to convey particular meanings, utilising as their sources their knowledge of the general properties of the linguistic system

and their sensitivity to the particular cultural and situational setting.

In the mid-1970s, Halliday took up the newly-founded Chair of Linguistics at the University of Sydney and was instrumental in supporting research initiatives in Australia, within the field of educational linguistics, which attempted to translate some of his theories into teaching practice. One of the most well-known and documented is the LERN Project in New South Wales, led by J R Martin, which investigated the textual demands of school literacy and identified 6 key genres: report, explanation, procedure, discussion, recount and narrative. The LERN Project established a 3-part Teaching/Learning Cycle in the shape of a wheel which has had considerable influence in establishing a pedagogy of genre literacy. The three stages of the wheel are: Modelling, Joint Negotiation of Text and Independent Construction of Text.

There is now a corpus of research and writing about genre theory and though there are disagreements amongst genre linguists (about the nature of language and the pedagogic applications of their ideas) there is a consensus on the underlying principles:

- the focus of genre is on whole texts, looking at the underlying purpose or function of the whole rather than on individual sentences
- genres are social processes given that texts are patterned in reasonably predictable ways according to patterns of social interaction in a particular culture
- genre analysis enables people to identify shared or generic features of texts which are produced with a common purpose and with a common context. These features relate to both the organisation of the text and linguistic patterns and conventions

- genre explores and recognises the differences between the grammar of writing and the grammar of speech and makes these explicit
- recognition of these generic features helps to empower individuals, enabling them to learn to manipulate the most powerful genres within contemporary society, opening up access not only to education but to social mobility.

The Application of Genre Theory in this Book

In producing this book, we were driven by an interest in the teaching of writing to ESOL and Basic Skills students and by the principles of genre theory that seemed applicable to our own experience. Indeed, much of what the genre theorists put forward is neither new nor original to them but has been practised, to some degree or other, by many teachers for a number of years. However, what was striking from reading the work of Gunther Kress, J R Martin, Joan Rothery and Frances Christie, and investigating the projects and INSET programmes they have inspired was the systematic approach to the collaborative analysis and discussion between teachers and students on the hows and whys of writing which is central to their approach. The formalisation of a generic process or method is one of the most compelling aspects of their educational contribution. In the early stages of preparation, we came across the work of David Wray and Maureen Lewis from the University of Exeter and the EXEL Project and their experience with writing frames. This too encouraged us to experiment with similar 'scaffolding' systems.

Genre versus traditionalist and process pedagogies

Genre theorists claim to represent a new educational paradigm, transcending both the traditionalist, 'back to basics' approach - with its emphasis on formal correctness, the learning of language 'facts' and its transmission pedagogy - and the progressive 'process' pedagogies which stress 'natural' learning through the doing of writing. Advocates of the latter have greeted genre literacy theory with considerable defensiveness, arguing that genre is formulaic and robs individuals of personal meaning in their writing. This, they claim, makes the writing disconnected from experience. Their view is that personal ownership is more important than linguistic and textual features, which they say fall into place with time. It is the message not the medium which is key to the process of writing. Genre theorists respond to these claims by pointing to the failure of progressive, 'process' pedagogies to improve patterns of educational attainment, making no real impact on improving access to social mobility through education for historically marginalised social groups.

Implications for Adult ESOL and Basic Skills students in Britain

It would seem to us that genre theory has something to offer practitioners in the field of ESOL and Basic Skills, though it may not be quite the messianic movement that some claim, particularly if it focuses entirely on schematic structures and posits generic models of correctness. Equally, there are many applications of the process approach to literacy we can use which support the development of student creativity and voice.

In producing this book we have found that a genre approach raises issues which are of particular relevance.

1   Genre gives students analytical tools to help them focus on narrative discourse features - the organisation of ideas, chronology, cohesion etc. - as well as generic language patterns and structures.

2   It makes explicit the cultural expectations encoded in certain types of writing.

3   It brings factual, as well as personal writing within the grasp of students who may have been away from formal education for some time or who never had the opportunity to gain the writing skills in the first place.

4   It makes explicit the differences between the grammar, lexis and register of spoken varieties of English as compared to that of Standard English in its written form.

5   Teachers can offer support through a 'scaffolded' process, whereby models of texts are put forward and jointly analysed through an inductive process. Students are then supported through a collaborative process to produce drafts, using writing frames where

appropriate. Finally, students produce their own individual texts based on personal experience and thought.

6   The use of writing frames is of particular value for dyslexic students who benefit greatly from the explicit nature of the structure the frames offer. Dyslexic students find value in a holistic, context bound approach where text organisation is given as much importance as other textual features.

7   The approach enables bilingual students to relate writing in English to writing in their own language, giving them opportunities to explore differences and similarities and to gain greater control of their authorship.

Further Reading

Cope B. & Kalantzis M. (eds) 1993 *The Powers of Literacy. A Genre Approach to Teaching Writing.* Falmer Press

Halliday M. A. K. 1975 *Learning How to Mean* London: E.Arnold

Huxley M. & Braddock L. March/April 1998 *Writing Using a First Steps Approach* The Primary English Magazine

Kay H. & Dudley-Evans A. October 1998 *Genre: what teachers think* ELT Journal Volume 52/4

Lewis M. & Wray D. 1995 *Developing Children's Non-fiction Writing* Leamington Spa: Scholastic

Lewis M. & Wray D. *Writing Frames* EXEL, Reading & Language Information Centre, University of Reading

Maybin J. & Stierer B. (eds) 1994 *Language, Literacy & Learning in Educational Practice* Multilingual Matters/Open University

Reid I. (ed) 1998 *The Place of Genre in Learning* Geelong: Deakin University

Vygotsky L. 1962 *Thought and Language* Cambridge Ma: MIT Press

Learning Unlimited

Learning Unlimited is a social enterprise that believes that learning should be empowering for individuals, communities and organisations. We work at local, regional, national and international levels to provide engaging, creative solutions to educational opportunities and challenges.

Learning Unlimited is taking forward the work of LLU+ and builds on a reputation for excellence, developed over 30 years, in the specialisms of literacy, language (ESOL and ELT), numeracy, family learning and teacher and trainer education.

We Offer:

exciting and creative teaching and training in a wide range of learning contexts

specialist knowledge and expertise in adult education

critical and innovative responses to educational

For more information, please contact:

Learning Unlimited
Institute of Education
20 Bedford Way
London WC1H 0AL
Tel: 020 7911 5561
Email: info@learningunlimited.co
Web: www.learningunlimited.co

About the Authors

Marina Spiegel was born in Argentina and has taught modern languages and ESOL. She has a particular interest in training and developing materials. She is co-author of Chart Your Course in English and Friends, Families and Folktales.

Helen Sunderland has always had a particular interest in teaching literacy skills and works as a teacher educator and consultant with a special interest in teaching bilingual learners and working with dyslexic learners. She is co-author of a number of publications including Dyslexia and the Bilingual Learner, Friends, Families and Folktales and The Teacher's Video: an ESOL Tutor Training Resource.

The authors also co-wrote:

Teaching Basic Literacy to ESOL Learners
Teaching Basic Literacy to ESOL Learners Support Pack
Writing Works: A genre approach